T0327845

THE
KOREAN MYTHS

THE
KOREAN MYTHS
A GUIDE TO THE GODS,
HEROES AND LEGENDS

HEINZ INSU FENKL
BELLA MYŎNG-WŎL DALTON-FENKL

To all our teachers.

A NOTE ON ROMANIZATION

This book uses the Revised Romanization of Korean system, also known as the Ministry of Culture system, which was developed by the National Academy of the Korean Language and officially adopted by the South Korean government in 2000. This system is thought to be more user-friendly and expedient than the McCune Reischauer system that is still used in Korean Studies scholarship because it doesn't require the use of special characters for diacritical marks. Since South Korea still uses Chinese characters (sinographs, called *hanja* in Korean), those are provided along with the phonetic Korean (*hangul*) spelling of significant names since they can provide underlying meanings and help to avoid ambiguity or confusion caused by varying Romanizations. Where they are relevant, literal translations of the meanings of names are also provided. When terms are provided in *hangul* and *hanja* with their Romanization but are not glossed, it is because they are simply 'name' characters that otherwise have no other reading.

HALF TITLE: A 10th-century gilt bronze rafter finial shaped like a dragon's head, which would have originally been attached to a royal hall or temple, early Goryeo dynasty.

FRONTISPIECE: A painted door panel from Haedong Yonggung Temple, Busan, depicting a dragon's head.

First published in the United Kingdom in 2024 by
Thames & Hudson Ltd, 181A High Holborn, London WC1V 7QX

First published in the United States of America in 2024 by
Thames & Hudson Inc., 500 Fifth Avenue, New York, New York 10110

The Korean Myths © 2024 Thames & Hudson Ltd, London

Text © 2024 Heinz Insu Fenkl and
Bella Myŏng-wŏl Dalton-Fenkl

Designed by P D Burgess

British Library Cataloguing-in-Publication Data
A catalogue record for this book is available from the British Library

Library of Congress Control Number 2024934744

ISBN 978-0-500-02766-0

Printed and bound in Slovenia by DZS-Grafik d.o.o.

Be the first to know about our new releases,
exclusive content and author events by visiting
thamesandhudson.com
thamesandhudsonusa.com
thamesandhudson.com.au

CONTENTS

Map 6

Introduction 8

1
Cosmogony and Other Origins 28

2
Religion in Korea 56

3
Ghosts, Spirits and Superstition 105

4
Central Themes in Folklore and Legend 132

5
North Korea: The Real Hermit Kingdom 154

6
Korea in the Modern Era 189

Timeline 227
Bibliography 230
Acknowledgments 233
Sources of Illustrations 235
Index 236

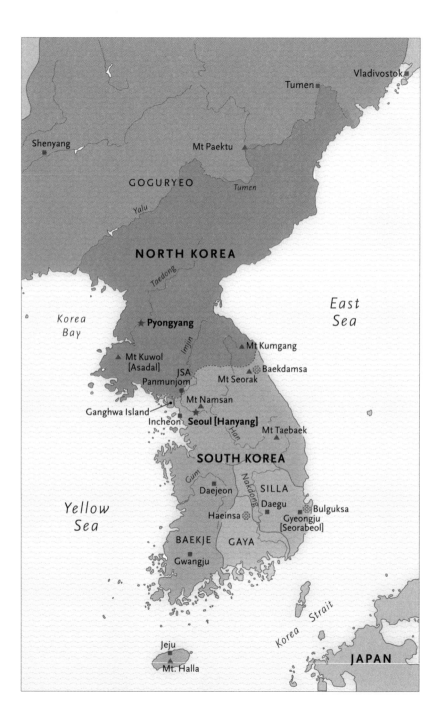

Key Events

c. 2333 BCE–108 BCE	Ancient Korea: Gojoseon (고조선/ 古朝鮮)
37 BCE–668 CE	The Three Kingdoms: Goguryeo (고구려/高句麗) Baekje (백제/百濟) and Silla (신라/新羅)
42–562 CE	Gaya (가야/伽倻)
668–935	Unified Silla
918–1392 1270–1356	Goryeo (고려/高麗); under Mongol rule
1392–1910	Joseon (조선/朝鮮)
1910	Korea is annexed by Japan
1945	Korea is liberated from Japanese rule
1945–1948	The Korean peninsula is divided along the 38th parallel
1948	The Republic of Korea (South Korea) and the Democratic People's Republic of Korea (North Korea) are established
1950–1953	The Korean War

MAP LEGEND

★ Capital cities

■ Major cities

▲ Major mountains

❀ Major Buddhist temples

From its tumultuous history, marked by competing kingdoms, foreign invasions and the Korean War, to its emergence as a global economic powerhouse and cultural trendsetter, South Korea stands as a testament to resilience and innovation in the delicate balance between tradition and modernity. Rapid industrialization and export-oriented growth policies – often adopted at the expense of political freedoms – propelled South Korea into the ranks of major global powers by the last decades of the twentieth century, and today it is home to multinational corporations like Samsung, Hyundai, Daewoo and LG. Political repression under its autocratic presidents and dictators has given way to authentic, though troubled, democratization, and the political engagement of the younger generation, coupled with a growing awareness of social issues, is shaping the country's democratic evolution. This journey from post-war devastation to world-leading dynamism, referred to as the 'Miracle on the Han River', is legendary. Today, South Korea holds the attention of the world.

By the mid-1980s, as South Korea eagerly anticipated hosting the 1988 Summer Olympic Games, the government had already begun a campaign of *gukjegyo* (국제교), or 'internationalization', with the idea that Korea would begin to export its culture in the same way it had been successfully exporting its material products. The ultimate goal was that Korea's culture would have an international prominence equivalent to its economy. *Gukjegyo* happens to sound almost identical to *gukjaegyo*, which means 'diplomatic bridge'. Taxi drivers would listen to daily English lessons on their radios as they drove their fares around Seoul in preparation for the Games. The number 88, or *palpal* (팔팔), became a craze – it was everywhere, from café and restaurant names to the logos of small manufacturing companies. *Palpal* sounds like the Korean sound effect for a rapid boil, and can mean 'feverish' or 'hard'. Korea was literally in the throes of '88 fever', and the long-term results of the nation's sponsorship of those Summer Games is still being seen today in the Korean Wave. K-Wave, or Hallyu, has become a global phenomenon, introducing the world to the country's pop culture, music, TV dramas and films. K-pop groups such as BTS and Blackpink have achieved unprecedented international success, drawing millions of fans worldwide. Korean dramas, known for their addictively compelling storylines and high production values, have also gained immense popularity, transcending cultural boundaries and language barriers – even proving that Americans will read subtitles. Hallyu has sparked worldwide interest in Korea's language, folklore and traditional culture.

Hallyu is a seemingly unstoppable tide of music and drama inundating the globe, and yet, ironically, it emerges from a place once called 'The Hermit Kingdom' for its wilful isolation from the outside world. This dynamic contradiction is one of the features that makes Korean culture and myth so fascinating. The two nations that currently occupy the Korean peninsula share a rich mythic tradition abounding with holy mountains, Shamanic shrines, supernatural creatures, and uneasy spirits. Tales of cunning heroes who trick unjust authority figures, tragic stories of mournful and vengeful ghosts, sons made heroes by their virtuous mothers, and filial daughters who sacrifice themselves for their families – all of these narratives resonate in a culture that blends Confucian, Taoist and

Buddhist philosophies with yet more ancient traditions, and these are the deep source of the contemporary Hallyu phenomenon. Myths remain very much a living and evolving part of Korean society.

The Korean peninsula is currently divided into two countries: the Republic of Korea and the Democratic People's Republic of Korea, known generally as South and North Korea respectively. This division resulted from the complex geopolitical dynamics preceding, and in the aftermath of, the Second World War: in 1945, the peninsula was divided along the 38th parallel into two zones, with the northern zone occupied by the Soviet Union and the southern zone occupied by the United States of America. Tensions between North and South Korea escalated, leading to the outbreak of the Korean War in 1950, when North Korean forces, backed by the Soviet Union and China, invaded South Korea. The Korean War devastated the entire peninsula, leaving nearly every major city in ruins and nearly three million civilians dead. It ended in an armistice in 1953, but no formal peace treaty was ever signed. Ironically, the countries were left divided along roughly the same 38th parallel as before the war, but the conflict had resulted in the separation of nearly ten million families, an added legacy of suffering. As a result, the Korean peninsula remains one of the most heavily militarized and politically tense regions in the world. But while the two Koreas are relatively young countries, with distinctly different political and economic systems, they share a cultural heritage that dates back nearly 5,000 years, including a common language and traditions, as well as a large body of mythology. Most of the discussion of Korean myths in this book will address 'Korea' as a whole, with its shared heritage, unless there is a particular reason to focus on either North or South Korea.

THE KOREAN PENINSULA

Korea's geology, geography and climate play a central role in its myths. Korea is one of the most mountainous countries in the world – over 70 per cent of the peninsula is covered in hills and mountains (though only a few are of high elevation). Because of this, much of Korea's mythology revolves around holy mountains. Korea also has a monsoon season, and flooding and landslides appear often in its myths and folk tales. The peninsula is also of strategic value – an old Korean proverb describes its position between greater powers as 'a shrimp between whales' – and rebellion and trickery in the face of powerful opposition are recurring themes in Korean stories.

An ancient map of Korea, created during the early Joseon dynasty, featuring Korea's eight provinces.

How a Korean Named America

When a great European mapmaker of ancient times was finishing his map of the Western hemisphere, he still didn't have a name for the continents there. He asked far and wide, until finally he came to a Korean. 'How should I name it?' he asked. The Korean was busy, as Koreans usually are. Annoyed, he snapped, 'Amureokkaena!', meaning 'However you want!'. The mapmaker, not knowing Korean, misheard. 'Amerika!' he said. 'What a wonderful name.' And that's why the continents in the Western hemisphere are called 'America'.

South Korea is situated in the southern part of the Korean peninsula and includes Ganghwa Island and Jeju Island, along with thousands of smaller islands. Its capital, Seoul, is one of the largest and most dynamic cities in the world. South Korea was established as a democratic republic in 1948 under the leadership of President Syngman Rhee (who was installed by the Americans), but its political history has been volatile. Syngman Rhee resigned in 1960, after widespread political protests due to his corruption, and General Park Chung-hee seized power in a military coup in 1961. Even as the country re-established democracy in the 1990s, accusations of corruption remained rife. Yet South Korea is now a thriving democracy with a market-oriented economy that has global influence and a strong emphasis on technology and industrial development.

North Korea is located in the part of the Korean peninsula north of the 38th parallel, where the Soviets had made amphibious landings the day before Japan's surrender in 1945, marking the complex political dynamics involved in the beginning of the separate histories of North and South Korea. Its capital is Pyongyang. North Korea is known for its authoritarian government, a de-facto military dictatorship led by the ruling Kim 'dynasty', which has been in power since the country's founding in 1948. Kim Il-sung, the first ruler, instituted an ideology of strict self-reliance even while the economy was actually based on heavy industry and agriculture in the Stalinist model with substantial aid from the Soviet Union and China. Well into the 1960s the general standard of living in the North was markedly better than in South Korea. But North Korea faced severe economic challenges after the collapse of the Soviet Union in the 1990s due to its stringent and self-imposed isolationism. Nonetheless, the Kim lineage is now in its third iteration, with Kim Jong-un (the 'Supreme Leader'), son of Kim Jong-il (the 'Dear Leader' and 'Guiding Star') and grandson of Kim Il-sung (the 'Sun of the Nation' and 'Eternal President'), in power. The country has a centralized economy that is controlled by its Communist Party, and is isolated from the rest of the world due to its closed political system and nuclear weapons programme, which it periodically wields as a threat to global security.

North Korean jurisdiction also extends to islands near the peninsula, including several islands in the Yalu River that runs between North Korea and China. Many foundational myths of Korea involve locations in North Korea, and the semi-mythical first Korean kingdom of Gojoseon extended north into what is now Manchuria. Over the millennia, the various kingdoms that occupied the Korean peninsula have gone by many different names, but since the founding of Joseon in the twelfth century only two general terms have been applied to Korea by Koreans.

Joseon (조선 / 朝鮮)

The Joseon dynasty was the last dynastic kingdom of Korea and included the House of Yi, which ruled the peninsula from 1392 to

1910. 'Joseon', which comes from the Chinese, literally means 'bright morning', which gave rise to the late nineteenth-century English appellation 'The Land of Morning Calm'. The first character, 朝, can also be read as 'towards', suggesting that the name might originally have designated a kingdom to the east, 'in the direction of morning'. The name Joseon is generally used to refer to both the dynasty and the period in Korean history encompassed by its rule.

In North Korea, 'Joseon' is used to refer to both Korea as a culture and Koreans as a people. North Koreans refer to themselves as *Joseon saram*, meaning 'Joseon people', although the official name for North Korea is *Joseon Minjujui Inmin Gonghwaguk* (조선민주주의인민공화국), The Democratic People's Republic of Korea. North Koreans call South Korea *Nam Joseon* (남조선), which means 'South Joseon'.

Hanguk (한국 / 韓國)

This is the modern South Korean name for the country, short for *Daehan Minguk* (대한민국 / 大韓民國), which literally means 'The Nation of the Great Han People' and is officially translated into English as 'The Republic of Korea'. The word Han (韓) is not the same as the one used for the Han (漢) dynasty or the Han people of China. South Koreans refer to themselves as *Hanguk saram* or *Hanguk in*, meaning 'Korean people'. They call South Korea *Namhan* (남한 / 南韓), literally 'South Han', and North Korea *Bukhan* (북한 / 北韓), literally 'North Han'.

Korea

The word 'Korea' is a foreign term derived from 'Goryeo', referring to the Goryeo dynasty, which ruled between 918 and 1392, prior to the Joseon dynasty. 'Goryeo' was formerly Romanized as Koryŏ or Koryeo, which eventually became the current spelling of Korea. The spelling was also influenced by the French term for Korea, 'Corée', which resulted, for a time, in the hybrid Anglicized spelling 'Corea' to align with the spelling of Joseon, which was formerly Romanized as Chosen, Chosŏn and Choseon at different times. Ethnic Koreans in Russia and Ukraine refer to themselves as *Koryo saram*, 'Koryo people'.

KING SEJONG THE GREAT AND *HANGUL*

King Sejong the Great (세종대왕 / 世宗大王, which can be read 'Noble Ancestor Great King') was the fourth king of the Joseon dynasty, reigning from 1418 to 1450, a period often called the 'Golden Age of Joseon'. He is widely regarded as one of the most influential and enlightened monarchs in Korean history, particularly known for his compassionate wisdom and his contributions to advancements in science, culture and the arts. Sejong also implemented legal reforms to ensure a fair and just legal system, establishing the Office of the Inspector General, which served to monitor and report corruption within the government.

Among all his achievements, King Sejong is best remembered for his leading role in the creation of *hangul*, the Korean phonetic alphabet, which is considered one of the most scientific and efficient writing systems in the world today. He introduced *hangul* in 1443 to promote literacy among the common people, because the existing writing system, Classical Chinese characters (*hanja*), was complex and not easily accessible to the general population. According to

Korean and Sino-Korean Etymology

Korean literature involves a great deal of complex and entertaining wordplay based on its dual use of the *hangul* and *hanja* systems. *Hangul* (the native script) is a phonetic alphabet, so each individual letter in *hangul* does not have a meaning on its own. The corresponding *hanja* (borrowed Chinese characters) are important because they allow one to see the underlying meaning of each individual character in the way Latin and Greek prefixes and suffixes in English may illuminate a word's meaning without having to rely on contextual cues. One Korean word for 'landscape' or 'scenery', for example, is *sansu*, rendered in *hangul* as 산수 and in *hanja* as 山水.

hangul	hanja	romanization
산수	山水	***sansu***

(mountain + water)

Both versions have the same pronunciation and are Romanized the same way. Another word, spelled identically, 산수 , but without corresponding *hanja*, means 'arithmetic', while yet another 산수 with the *hanja* 山獸 has the literal reading of 'mountain animal' and means 'wild animal', though it is also spelled 산수 in *hangul* and also Romanized as *sansu*.

legend, King Sejong struggled for years to come up with the shapes of the letters until one night, when he was exhausted, he noticed the geometric shapes in the wooden frame of his rice-paper door panels. In a eureka moment, he realized those shapes would be familiar to everyone and adopted them as the basic structure of the Korean alphabet. Another legend suggests that a young scholar (or one of King Sejong's children), concerned about the king's health, helped him by painting the shapes of the letters with honey onto the rice paper of the door panels. When insects ate the sweet paper,

A statue of King Sejong the Great, Gwanghwamun Plaza, Seoul. See p. 136 for an equally famous statue in the same plaza.

they left the letter forms as holes in the paper. The king took that as a divine sign and used the shapes for *hangul*.

Hangul, which was the product of many years of research and development both by King Sejong himself and members of his Hall of Worthies (the royal research institute he established), is so efficient that the saying goes: 'An intelligent man can learn it in a day and even a fool can learn it in ten.' This is precisely why the new writing system was initially denigrated by the literate upper class: it was too easy to learn and could pose political problems by creating an educated peasantry. It was called the 'vulgar script', the 'children's script', and even the 'women's script'. *Hangul* was actually banned in 1504 by Yeonsangun (who is widely considered the worst ruler in Korean history), when commoners used it to mock him, but it was kept alive by women, Buddhist monks, and later by Christians. It continued to gain popularity over the years, until it was adopted as

A page of the *Hunminjeongeum*, a 1446 book explaining *hangul's* creation and its logic. This title was also the old name of *hangul* itself.

Korea's official writing system in the mid-1800s. *Hangul* was banned once again in 1910 when Korea was colonized by the Japanese, and it became a symbol of Korean identity and subversion until Korea's liberation from Japan in 1945.

WHAT IS MYTH?

For the purposes of this book, 'myth' will refer to more than the traditional, scholarly definition of the word. In common speech, people often group myth, legend and folklore together instead of adhering strictly to their definitions, and the authors of this book want to reflect this fact and to offer a broader insight into the ideas that shape Korean culture. Nationalistic propaganda that bleeds into the mythic will also be discussed. That being said, it is also useful to know what separates these terms and categories from one another.

A myth is a traditional or sacred story, typically of ancient origin, that explains the beliefs, practices, customs or natural phenomena of a society or culture. Myths often feature gods, supernatural beings or legendary heroes, and are typically passed down from one generation to the next through the oral tradition. This means they are not necessarily written down, but are shared through storytelling within a community or culture.

Myths serve various purposes within a culture or society. These can include explaining natural phenomena – myths often provide explanations for natural events or features of the world, such as the origin of the stars, the changing of seasons, or the creation of specific geographical landmarks. Myths also frequently convey moral lessons or cultural values. They may illustrate desired behaviours and moral virtues, or consequences of certain actions. These stories can be used to reinforce societal norms and ethics. In a similar vein, myths can legitimize the authority of rulers, leaders or institutions by claiming divine or supernatural validation. Myths can also help preserve a culture's identity by narrating its history, origins and unique characteristics, and they often reinforce a sense of shared heritage among a people. Finally, some myths simply provide entertainment with narratives that captivate audiences with their imaginative characters, adventures and mysteries.

In colloquial usage, the term 'myth' is also used to describe a widely held but false or exaggerated belief, story or idea – something that is commonly accepted or repeated, even though it may not be based on factual evidence. In this sense, people might say that something is a 'myth' to indicate that it is a misconception, a fallacy, or a popular but untrue notion. In this book, we are rarely using myth in terms of this meaning of the word, unless discussing a popular notion or belief that is nonetheless revealing about Korean culture in underlying ways. We explore how myths often tell us a

A Joseon-era folk painting of a tiger and magpies, a frequent subject of Korean paintings, pairing and contrasting the cleverness of the magpies with the authority and power of the tigers.

great deal about Korean history and culture, whether or not their substance is literally true.

Like a myth, a legend is a traditional narrative or story that is passed down through generations via the oral tradition. Legends, however, are typically based on real historical people, places or events, though these may have been embellished or distorted over time through the telling. They often contain elements of the super-natural, heroic feats or extraordinary events. Legends are typically culturally significant, serving moral or educational purposes. They can convey lessons, values or warnings, and they may reinforce a group's identity or worldview. They often blur the line between fact and fiction. They incorporate supernatural or miraculous elements that challenge strict realism, but they may contain a kernel of truth, especially when they are origin tales.

Folklore refers to the collective knowledge and creative expres-sions of a community and reflects the values, traditions and identity of that group. It encompasses both myth and legend, as well as folk tales, proverbs and riddles, but also includes non-narrative elements, such as songs, dances, rituals and customs. These traditional beliefs, stories and customs are typically passed down informally through generations of a close-knit community, either orally or through other mediums, like songs, dances and visual arts. Folklore plays a vital role in preserving and expressing the cultural identity of a community or group. It reflects the shared history, values and world-view of that community. It is defined by adaptation and continuity (i.e. 'living' tradition) – folklore is not static, rather evolving over time as it is adapted to changing social, cultural and historical contexts. Despite such adaptations, it often maintains a sense of continuity and connection to the past. Examples of folklore include urban legends, traditional folk songs, children's games, playground rhymes, jokes, creation myths, superstitions, fairy tales, and the customs associated with holidays and festivals.

MYTH AND RELIGION

In a religious context, myths often serve as explanatory narratives that help believers understand the origins of their faith, the nature of the divine, and the moral and ethical principles that guide their lives. Likewise, from a secular point of view, myths that originate in a religious tradition offer insight into that worldview. Since myths are so deeply intertwined with religious beliefs and practices, and are often vehicles for expressing religious and philosophical ideas, knowing the religious background of a culture or tradition – particularly one as complex as Korea's – can help decipher the symbolic and metaphorical aspects of myths, allowing a fuller understanding of what they convey.

What is Syncretism?

'Syncretism' refers to an amalgamation or fusing of different ideas and traditions. Korea's myths and religions have been syncretic for many centuries, as newer faiths adapt the ideas of older faiths and indigenous traditions incorporate elements of the new religions. At different times throughout Korean history, the dominant religious or political institutions, as well as colonial powers, have attempted to suppress traditions such as Shamanism, Christianity and Buddhism, but Koreans have always fought to keep their belief systems alive.

It is important to note that many Koreans incorporate elements of multiple belief systems into their spiritual practices. For example, some people may follow Buddhist traditions while also participating in Confucian rituals and celebrating Christmas. Korea, in general, has a dynamic and diverse religious landscape, and there are several significant religions and belief systems practised throughout the peninsula. Even in North Korea, where the state ideology is anti-religious, there is tolerance of Buddhist practice and a recognition of the indigenous religion of Cheondogyo, as well as a small number of Christians. North Korea is also, in many ways, a new kind of theocracy in which adulation of the Kim lineage is tantamount to religious practice and resonates with myths from other traditions like Taoism and Shamanism. Korea, as a whole, exhibits a high degree of syncretism – that is, the blending of different religious traditions – in its religious practices, and so its myths also tend to be complex expressions of syncretism.

For these reasons, it is necessary to briefly contextualize the religious traditions before presenting myths that may be derived from or influenced by them (a more detailed discussion of Korea's religions follows in Chapter 2). The major religions in South Korea are summarized below, with approximate percentages based on estimates from a 2021 Gallup Korea poll, though note that Confucianism is not currently classified as a religion in Korea and that Shamanism has, over the years, been shifted to the 'no religion' category for political reasons.

Shamanism

Shamanism is indigenous to Korea and has been an integral part of Korean culture since Neolithic times (8000 to 1400 BCE). Although it has sharply declined in prominence compared to the past, Shamanic rituals and beliefs still permeate the national consciousness. Since Shamanism has always readily incorporated elements of other traditions, it has adapted to recent innovations in technology and is now a thriving part of the internet culture in Korea.

Taoism

Taoism was also brought to Korea via China, around the seventh century, and while it never established itself as a major institutional religion, its philosophical ideas, aesthetic ideals, meditative

Taegeukgi, the Korean Flag

The deep influence of Taoist philosophy in Korean culture can easily be seen in the design of the South Korean flag, called the *Taegeukgi* (태극기). The *taegeuk*, a traditional Korean symbol representing the Taoist concepts of dualism, balance and harmony, has featured on the flag in various forms since ancient times.

Between 1910 and 1945, when Korea was under Japanese colonial rule, the use of the *Taegeukgi* was prohibited and severely punished – the Japanese flag was used in all Korean public spaces. It was not until after Korea's liberation at the end of the Second World War that the country was able to reassert its national identity. The current flag of South Korea was officially adopted on 15 October 1949. The *taegeuk*, a swirling circle with a light half (yang) and a dark half (yin), is surrounded by four trigrams from the *I Ching* (see p. 41). Each trigram symbolizes one of the four cardinal elements and represents various natural forces and concepts:

☰ (*Geon* / 건) Heaven, air, father, spring, east.
☷ (*Gon* / 곤) Moon, water, daughter, winter, north.
☵ (*Gam* / 감) Sun, fire, son, autumn, south.
☳ (*Lee* / 리) Earth, mother, summer, west.

practices and medical knowledge are deeply integrated into Korean culture. There are few Taoist temples in Korea, but Taoist shrines and deities can be found among Shamanic shrines and are commonplace in Korean folklore. The symbolism of the flag of South Korea, with its *taegeuk* and trigrams, is a prime example of Taoist influence.

Confucianism

Confucianism was introduced to Korea from China in the late thirteenth century and has been the dominant cultural tradition for the past 500 years; it is not without reason that Korea is considered the

The Yi dynasty (Joseon era) royal flag showing all eight trigrams, 1882–1907.

Flag of the Korean Empire from the same era and precursor to the modern flag.

The white background of the flag, which is said to be derived from the traditional Korean clothing called *hanbok*, symbolizes purity, peace and the desire for unification between North and South Korea. The *Taegeukgi* embodies the Korean philosophy of *Hongik Ingan* (홍익인간), which means 'for the benefit of all humanity'. It is not only a representation of South Korea's national identity – the state – but also a symbol of Korea's cultural identity and the people themselves. For this reason, there are very few incidents of its desecration even during violent political protests.

most Confucian nation in the world. While not typically classified as a religion, Confucianism permeates all aspects of Korean life and has tremendous influence on education, ethical and moral values and social hierarchy (particularly gender hierarchy).

Buddhism

Buddhism was brought to Korea in the fourth century CE and flourished in the 'golden age' of the Great Silla period (668–935), but was

A late Joseon-dynasty hanging scroll of Gwanseeum, a key deity in Korean Buddhism. A Dragon King is in the bottom left corner and a buddha in each upper corner.

actively suppressed during the subsequent Joseon era (1392–1910). Buddhism went through a revival after the Korean War and, until the past decade, when a growing number of South Koreans have begun to identify as non-religious or secular, was one of the dominant religious traditions in Korea; 16 per cent of Koreans identified as Buddhist in the 2021 poll, while 60 per cent identified with 'no religion', many of them from the younger generation. Buddhist temples can be found throughout Korea (even in the North). The Jogye Order, a Seon (Zen) sect, is the largest.

Christianity

Catholicism was introduced into Korea via China in the early eighteenth century, and Protestantism was brought by missionaries towards the end of the nineteenth century. In the twentieth century, while the number of Catholics declined, Korea was considered a tremendous success story for Protestantism, which grew rapidly and became a significant political force after democratization in the 1990s. Today, the number of missionaries Korea sends into the world is second only to the United States, and 25 per cent of Koreans identify as Christian (17 per cent Protestant, 6 per cent Catholic).

COSMOGONY AND OTHER ORIGINS

THE CREATION MYTHS

Cosmological myths typically describe the fundamental origins of things: light out of darkness; order out of chaos; the creation of the universe, the Earth and the heavenly bodies. The ancient peoples of Korea told various cosmological origin stories, first passed down through the oral tradition and eventually put down in writing. These narratives, which provide explanations for the origins of the world, humanity and natural phenomena, tend to vary by region. Interestingly, the ones that recount the creation of the world are not to be found in historical documents, but rather in the still-thriving oral traditions of shamans that reach back into antiquity and were recorded only in relatively recent times. The best known of these are *muga*, or 'shamans' songs', from the opposite ends – the most northern and most southern parts – of Korea.

The *Changsega* (창세가 / 創世歌)

The *Changsega* ('Song of Creation') is a shamans' song from the northern province of Hamgyeong that recounts the creation of the world and human beings. It is likely to be a variant of an older song, with the names of the divine figures – Mireuk (미륵 / 彌勒) and Seokga (석가 / 釋迦) – changed sometime after the introduction of Buddhism into Korea. Mireuk and Seokga are both buddhas in the Mahayana tradition, which is the dominant form of Buddhism in Korea. Seokga is the Korean form of Shakyamuni, the historic Buddha (Siddhartha Gautama) who founded the religion, and Mireuk is the Korean name for Maitreya, the future Buddha who does not yet exist in this world because he will only be born into it after the teachings of the original Buddha are lost. It may seem odd that a shaman's song, and particularly one as important as a creation narrative, would feature Buddhist figures as its primary actors, but this is typical of the religious syncretism characteristic of Korean Shamanism. A version of the story recorded in 1923 told by Kim Ssangdol, a great *manshin* (a shaman who could be possessed by spirits, see p. 61), goes as follows.

Long ago, heaven and earth were one thing, with no space in between for a world to exist. Then, one day, a crack appeared between the two, and the god Mireuk (Maitreya) placed copper pillars in the four directions to keep sky and earth apart. At the time, there were two suns and two moons, so Mireuk took one sun and one moon and formed the stars and constellations, the moon becoming the Big Dipper and the seven stars of the South and the sun becoming the small and large stars that are the destinies of common people and kings. There was arrowroot growing everywhere, stretching from mountain to mountain, so he cut it down and made himself a hempen robe and a hood.

There was no fire at the time and everything was eaten raw. Mireuk set out to find fire and water. First, he asked the grasshopper where he could find them, and the grasshopper said, 'How would I know? I drink dew at night and eat sunlight by day. Go ask the frog.' So Mireuk asked the frog and the frog said, 'I don't know. Ask the mouse.' When Mireuk asked the mouse, the mouse said, 'What

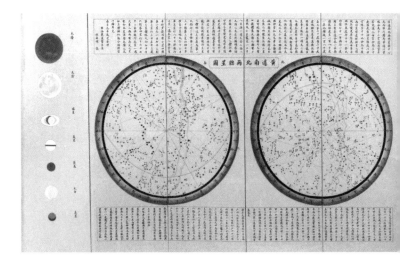

will you give me in return?' 'I will give you entrance to all the granaries in the world', answered Mireuk. So the mouse told him: 'Go to Mount Gumjeong. There you will find stone and iron. Hit them together and it will make fire. Then go to Mount Sohwa, and you will see water.' So Mireuk went to the top of Mount Gumjeong and made sparks and fire by striking quartz against pig iron. From Mount Sohwa he saw something shimmering, stretching out into the distance. That is how he found rivers, lakes and the ocean.

Mireuk was lonely in the world, so he held a gold tray in one hand and a silver tray in the other, and prayed to heaven. Five caterpillars came down onto each tray, the ones on the gold tray growing into men and the ones on the silver tray becoming women. These humans kept him company and populated the world. Everything was peaceful. But when the god Seokga (Shakyamuni) saw all

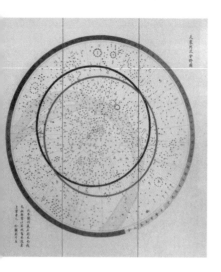

Restored versions of new (17th-century on the left) and old (14th-century on the right) astronomical charts, featuring stars, planets and moons. Originally these charts were all part of one eight-panel folding screen created in the 18th century.

this, he was envious of Mireuk, and wanted his time as ruler of the world to end. So Seokga challenged Mireuk to a series of contests. First, they competed to see who could draw more water from the East Sea. Mireuk won. Next, Seokga challenged him to freeze the Seongcheong River in summer; again, Mireuk won. Now Seokga proposed a third contest. He said, 'Let us sleep. If a peony blooms from my body, then the world is mine. If it blooms from yours, then the world is yours.' Mireuk fell into a deep sleep and a peony bloomed in his lap, but Seokga, who slept fitfully like a thief, had no flower. He plucked Mireuk's flower and put it in his own lap, thus winning the contest. Mireuk honoured the agreement and left the world under Seokga's rule, but he cursed Seokga for his trickery, saying, 'You have brought evil and suffering into this world.' He told him how every village would have shamans, courtesans and butchers – people of the despised class – and that 3,000 Buddhist monks and a thousand hermits would appear. Seokga's time would be the final age.

When the monks appeared three days later, Seokga took them to a mountain and caught deer, skewered their meat, cooked it, and fed it to the monks. But two of the monks would not eat the meat – they were truly holy men. When they died they became the rocks and pine trees on every mountain, and that is why they are still honoured in the springtime today.

At first glance, the use of the names of the Buddhas may seem to honour Buddhism, but it is clear that Seokga is the villain of the story, responsible for the ills of the world. Given that Buddhists historically denigrated and oppressed Shamanic practices (see p. 62), it is understandable that shamans would attribute suffering to the founding figure of Buddhism. It also makes sense on another level: Seokga is the one who formulated the Four Noble Truths, the fundamental

A 17th-century lacquer clothing box with a peony motif, decorated with mother-of-pearl. Lacquerware is a traditional Korean artform.

precepts upon which Buddhist philosophy and religion are based and the first of which is the truth of *dukka*, typically translated to mean that suffering is the natural condition of life. Thus the shamans cast Seokga as the literal originator of suffering, while casting Mireuk – who is described in Buddhism as being the future Buddha – as the protagonist, because he will only appear after the originator of suffering is gone. (Many Korean Buddhists await the coming of Mireuk in the same way that Evangelical Christians await the second coming of Christ and Jews await the Messiah, maybe not realizing that – according to their own Buddhist teachings – the Maitreya will not appear as long as there are Buddhists to await him!) The use of these Buddhist names in their creation story demonstrates the adaptability and the expedient cleverness of Korea's Shamanic tradition.

The *Cheonjiwang Bonpuri* (천지왕본풀이 / 天地王本풀이)

The *Cheonjiwang Bonpuri* ('The Origin Story of the King of Heaven and Earth') is a shamans' song from Jeju, the island that marks the ultimate southern reaches of Korea. There are many variants of this narrative, because it is still part of a living tradition and shamans adapt it – adding or subtracting details, making it longer or shorter – for the purposes of particular rituals.

Like the *Changsega* from Hamgyeong Province, the longer variant of the story begins with the creation of the world. In the beginning, everything was a vast and empty uniform void and heaven and earth were one. Then a hole formed in the void, and the light elements rose through it and the heavy elements fell into it, forming the sky and the earth. A bright dewdrop descended from heaven and a dark dewdrop rose from the earth and they swirled together, forming

Peonies and butterflies painted on silk fabric. Peonies have long been considered the 'king' of flowers in Korea and were a Joseon-era symbol of royalty.

everything but the sun, the moon and the stars. Then the three Rooster Kings of the sky, the earth and the human world all crowed. That is when time began and Cheonjiwang (천지왕 / 天地王), the King of Heaven and Earth, appeared. Cheonjiwang saw that the world was dark because there was no sun, and so he made two suns and two moons.

At this point the story goes off on a long digression, with details taken from Chinese folk literature, in which Cheonjiwang is at war with a figure named Sumyeong Jangja (壽命長子 / 수명장자). This is the tyrannical ruler of the human world, whose name means 'Long-lived Lord' and is said to have lived for 3,800 years. The arrogant Sumyeong Jangja, full of hubris, tried to depose Cheonjiwang, but he was defeated by 40,000 divine troops led by the generals of the elements thunder, lightning, fire, rain and wind. Cheonjiwang spared Sumyeong Jangja's life, and before returning to his heavenly realm on his chariot, he remained on earth for four days and four nights, during which he impregnated a beautiful and wise woman, Lady Chongmyeong (聰明 / 총명, 'Clever Brightness').

Two sons were born to Lady Chongmyeong: Daebyeol (대별 / 大별, 'Great Star') and Sobyeol (소별 / 小별, 'Little Star'). When they were old enough, she told them that their father was the King of Heaven and Earth, and that they may visit him by sowing the magical seeds he had left for them. The brothers planted the seeds and climbed up the squash vines that sprouted and reached all the way up into the heavenly realm. There, they met Cheonjiwang, who assigned the rulership of the human world to Daebyeol and the rulership of the underworld to Sobyeol.

But Sobyeol was jealous of Daebyeol. He did not want to rule the underworld, so he pleaded with his father, who came up with the contest of growing flowers. Sobyeol's flowers would not grow, but he won the contest through trickery by stealing Daebyeol's flowers while he was asleep. With his older brother now relegated to the under-world, Sobyeol went on a rampage, creating chaos in the terrestrial world. He defeated Sumyeong Jangja, who had continued to rule after being spared by Cheonjiwang. Sobyeol was less merciful than his father: he burned down Sumyeong Jangja's palace and dismembered him, scattering his remains, which became vermin, throughout the world. He even murdered Sumyeong Jangja's children; his son then became a bird of prey and his daughter became a bean weevil.

Because of Sobyeol's evil deeds, all the living things in the world began to speak, clamouring in protest at what he had done. Humans could hardly understand each other because they could not distin-guish their own voices from the voices of ghosts. The world became a violent and immoral place, made burning hot by the two suns in the day and freezing cold by the two moons at night. To bring the world back to order, Sobyeol finally appealed to his older brother for help.

Daebyeol came up from the underworld and shot an arrow into one of the suns and one of the moons, turning them into the stars of the eastern and western skies. He sprinkled the dust of pine bark onto plants and the tongues of animals, making them incapable of human speech. He separated humans from ghosts by weight, making them distinguishable from each other. But Sobyeol had not mentioned anything about the immorality of humans, and so Daebyeol did not correct the social order. That is why society is still corrupt and full of discord: lying, theft, treachery and adultery.

It is likely that the names of the principal characters in the *Cheonjiwang Bonpuri* are older than those of the *Changsega*, because they follow the ancient practice of naming characters for their roles

– Cheonjiwang literally translates as 'King of Heaven and Earth'. The presence of the pre-Buddhist figure, the King of Heaven and Earth himself, as opposed to a name borrowed from a Buddhist figure also seems to make it an older variant, and would explain who Mireuk prayed to in the *Changsega*.

The *Cheonjiwang Bonpuri* also introduces the theme of a father god and sibling rivalry, keeping the narrative focused on that of a divine family instead of introducing two figures from a foreign religion, suggesting it is more in keeping with Korea's Shamanic origins. Because of the pervasive influence of Confucianism and its preoccupation with lineage and hierarchy, sibling rivalry became a major theme throughout Korean folk tales.

Grandma Mago (마고할미) and Grandma Seolmundae (설문대할망)

The two stories recounted above, though usually sung by female shamans, centred around male protagonists. But in both the Jeju Island tradition and that of the peninsula, there are creation narratives that are widely known in the oral tradition even though they are not usually included in ritual performances or historical texts. They are most likely omitted from those canons because they privilege a female goddess, who wields the power to create the world with her own body. In the northern tradition, the giant Grandma Mago (Magohalmi) carried mud around in her skirts, and the places where she dumped it became mountains and islands. When she relieved herself, her urine became rivers and her faeces became hills. When she straddled mountains, the spray of her urine was so powerful that it cracked the boulders below. She was so huge that she could walk across the sea by stepping from island to island.

A holy tree with Shamanic talismans hanging from its branches and stones piled in front.

Grandma Seolmundae (Seolmundaehalmang, also known in ancient records as Seolmago) of the Jeju tradition is another giant goddess. She passed gas while she was sleeping and caused a chain of explosions that created the universe. She put out the plumes of fire that erupted from the sea by scooping mud from the sea floor and piling it up to create Jeju Island out of the volcanic mountain. Her urine caused a piece of the island to split off into a smaller island, Soseom. Grandma Seolmundae's body was the fertile earth, and her hair was the grass and trees. Her urine fertilized the ocean floor, giving rise to the bounties of the sea that the Jeju women divers harvested. The ocean surf was created by the shuffling of her feet, and when she strode through the sea it gave rise to fierce storms. But despite her size, she was unable to build a bridge to join the island to the peninsula, and despite her height, the bottomless pool in the crater of Mount Halla (the shield volcano on the island) was too deep for her, and that is where she drowned.

In another version of the Grandma Seolmundae story, she gives birth to five hundred sons and sends them out into the world to find food. In the meantime, she uses the crater in Mount Halla as a cauldron to make soup, but she accidentally falls in and drowns. When the sons return and eat the delicious soup, one of them finds her bones in the bottom of his bowl.

Two *dol hareubang* (돌 하르방, meaning 'stone grandpa') carved from basalt of Jeju Island. These statues likely had a Shamanic meaning.

Amusing Origins

Origin stories are not just limited to those from antiquity, nor are they always religious in nature – or even serious. They crop up constantly in the oral tradition, and some are more enduring than others. Below are two from the 1960s, from the town of Bupyeong, outside a major US military base, that show the influence of increasing Western presence in Korea following the Korean War years (1950–53).

The Origin of the Korean Complexion

When Hananim first made people out of clay, he baked them too long and they came out too dark. He tried again, and this time they didn't bake long enough, and they came out too white. Finally, on the third try, he baked the clay just right. That is the colour of the Korean people.

Why Koreans Have Flatter Noses than Caucasians

A long time ago, a Korean and a Caucasian got into an argument. They started fighting and grabbed whatever weapon they had on hand. The Caucasian happened to have a mallet, and he pounded the Korean's nose with it, making it flat. The Korean had a pair of tongs, and he grabbed the Caucasian's nose with them and pulled with all his might. That's why Koreans have flat noses and Caucasians have long noses, and are called *ppaenko* – 'pulled-out nose'.

FOUNDATION MYTHS

While there are relatively few Korean myths about the creation of the world and those who live in it, there are many accounts devoted to the founding of kingdoms and their ruling clans. Unlike the creation myths, which as we have seen were largely passed down through oral storytelling and shamans' songs, the main Korean foundation myths have been well documented in historical texts. Such accounts feature recurring central themes even while they may be about competing kingdoms. Because Korea has four major religious traditions, these foundation myths are also occasionally coloured by religious ideas that were imported from other parts of the world. The influence and practice of Taoism and Buddhism in Korea will be discussed at greater length in Chapter 2; here we will focus on the 'native' Korean foundation myths.

The two most important texts that provide insights into the early history of Korea are the *Samguk Sagi* ('History of the Three Kingdoms') and the *Samguk Yusa* ('Memorabilia of the Three Kingdoms'). They are very different texts, each with its distinct characteristics and purposes, and the two complement each other in providing an understanding of Korea's early history. The *Samguk Yusa* offers a blend of historical accounts, legends and religious beliefs, shedding light on the cultural and religious practices of the period. It was not compiled until the thirteenth century by the Buddhist monk Iryeon (1206–1289), and consequently features prominent Buddhist tropes. The first volume of the *Samguk Yusa* even includes a variant explanation for the origin of the *Zhou Yi* (or *I Ching*, 'Book of Changes', usually classified as a Chinese Taoist text), in which it is created by the half-serpent hero/deity Fuxi. On the other hand, the *Samguk Sagi* presents a more factual and political account, emphasizing political events, alliances and military affairs. Neither text, by today's academic standards, would be classified as histories because of their lack of objectivity and their underlying political agendas, and yet that is also why they are interesting. Considering the two in their own historical trajectories also provides some interesting insights into their respective agendas.

The *Samguk Sagi* (삼국사기 / 三國史記)

The *Samguk Sagi* ('History of the Three Kingdoms') is an official historical record of the Three Kingdoms period and the subsequent Unified Silla period, and the oldest surviving record of Korean history. It was commissioned by King Injong of Goryeo (r. 1122–1146) and compiled by a group of scholars led by Kim Busik, a historian and government official, in the mid-twelfth century. The primary objective of the *Samguk Sagi* was to provide a comprehensive and authoritative historical account of the period.

The *Samguk Sagi* draws on earlier historical records, official documents and first-hand accounts to provide what was, for its time, an attempt at an objective view of history. Its focus is primarily on political and military events, including the rise and fall of kingdoms, wars and diplomatic activities. It also provides detailed information about the ruling families, their alliances, and the power struggles among them.

Unlike the later *Samguk Yusa*, the *Samguk Sagi* leaves out mythical or religious elements and concentrates on the political and socio-economic aspects of the era. Nevertheless, one has to keep in mind that its objectivity, by today's standards, is questionable because of the writing practices of those times. The *Samguk Sagi* was modelled on earlier Chinese histories, which are famous for their selective use of detail, distortion, and sometimes outright falsehoods. (Confucius, for example, was known for rewriting earlier historical records to favour his patrons and cast those he did not like in an unfavourable light, or elide them altogether.) Kim Busik, though he was a Buddhist, compiled the *Samguk Sagi* in a way that emphasized and idealized Confucian virtues.

The *Samguk Yusa* (삼국유사 / 三國遺事)

The *Samguk Yusa* is a collection of legends, myths and historical accounts compiled by the Buddhist monk Iryeon during the reign of King Chungnyeol (충렬 / 忠烈, literally meaning 'fiercely honest/devoted') of Goryeo (1274–1308). The contents of the *Samguk Yusa* may be so different from its predecessor in part because it was written during the Mongol invasion. King Chungnyeol had been forced to marry a daughter of Kublai Khan, and was thus his son-in-law. While previous Korean rulers had been given their own unique titles for the purposes of veneration (e.g. Chumo the Holy), Chungnyeol was the first to bear the demoted title of *wang* (王), which means 'king', but which the Chinese considered closer to our definition of 'prince'. This was to make it clear that Korea was a subordinate, vassal state to the Mongol empire. (Later in the nineteenth century, when a Korean king was tricked into declaring himself emperor, that insult to China ultimately made Korea vulnerable to annexation by Japan.)

The *Samguk Yusa*, like the *Samguk Sagi*, covers the period from the Three Kingdoms (Goguryeo, Baekje and Silla) to Unified Silla, but given the political climate, one can see why Iryeon, a monk, was concerned for the preservation of Korean culture and religion. Thus, the primary purpose of the *Samguk Yusa* was likely to create a record of the traditions of the time, and to help unify the Korean people, who were suffering under the Mongols.

The 'Record of Great Wonders', which includes the first two of the nine parts in the *Samguk Yusa*, is especially fascinating. It features various mythical and legendary stories related to the founding of the kingdoms, the divine origins of kings, and other 'wondrous' tales with supernatural elements. As a monk, Iryeon infused Buddhist

The Otter and the Hunter

The enduring resonance of the strange stories from the
Samguk Yusa can be seen in this Zen prose poem by Musan Cho
Oh-hyun (무산 조오현 / 霧山 曺五鉉 1932–2018), from his collection
Tales from the Temple. During his later years, Master Cho served as
abbot of Baekdamsa, one of Korea's largest and oldest Buddhist
temples. Having come from humble roots, he was known for
emphasizing the theme of compassion in his literary work.
He retells the story, which is part of a longer narrative about
the great monk Hyetong, in a single, long, sentence:

A young hunter caught an otter that had come out to the water's
edge in search of food and he skinned it and strutted home with its
pelt, and the next day he noticed that the otter's bones – which he
had thrown away – had left bloody tracks walking off, and so he
cautiously followed the trail of blood into a cave, and inside the dark
cave he saw the heap of the thin bones that was the mother otter
he had skinned and flensed the day before still alive, and she was
embracing her five tiny pups – which had not yet opened their eyes
– and they couldn't see their mother's condition, and they were
mewling for milk, and the hunter was as cruel as a man could be,
but upon seeing the mother and her pups he could not help
himself, and so he took the place of the mother otter until the pups
were grown; he spent three years like that – which felt to him like
three eons – entirely cutting off the paths of the world and the
vagaries of the mind, and the only place someone like him could
go after that was to a Buddhist temple, and the temple refused him
because of the gamey odour that exuded from his body, and so he
stood in the yard with a brazier of burning charcoal on his head till
the crown of his head exploded with a sound like a thunderclap,
and only then did the head monk, whose name was Muwoe, heal
his wounds with a special mantra, giving him a reason to live and –
they say – bestowing upon him the name Hyetong. And all this
happened during the reign of King Munmu of Silla.

elements into the historical accounts, emphasizing the role of Buddhism in shaping Korean history and society. Interestingly, Iryeon cites now-lost Chinese sources, such as the *Wei-shu* ('History of the Wei Dynasty') and the *Dangun Gogi* ('Ancient Record of Tangun'), for some of the most important narratives, showing that the history of Korea he recounts was already known beyond the peninsula.

Because the *Samguk Yusa* provides valuable insights into the religious practices, rituals and cultural customs of ancient Korea, including folklore, legends and biographies of notable individuals, it is a more popular text – even among most scholars – than the *Samguk Sagi*, which is a much drier read. Over the years, countless movies, TV dramas and numerous comic book adaptations have been based on stories from the *Samguk Yusa* and serve as evidence of its continued influence on the Korean popular imagination. One of the most prominent of these was the 2010 historical drama *The King of Legend* (*Geunchogowang*, 근초고왕 / 近肖古王, literally 'High King Geuncho'), which was based not only on the historical information in the *Samguk Yusa* and *Samguk Sagi* but also on the novel *Han of the Continent* (*Daeryugui Han*, 대륙의 한) by Yi Mun-yol, one of South Korea's most important writers, also based on those two texts.

THE GREAT MYTHIC KINGS

The following three tales of mythic rulers of Korea are from the *Samguk Yusa* ('Memorabilia of the Three Kingdoms'), which is one of the primary sources of ancient Korean history.

Dangun, the First King of Korea

With only very minor variations between different versions of the story, what follows here is the story of how Korea's first king, known as Dangun ('Sandalwood King') or Dangun Wangeom (단군왕검 / 檀君王儉), was born.

The Lord of Heaven, Hwanin (환인 / 桓因), had a son named Hwanung (환웅 / 桓雄, 'Heavenly Hero'), who wanted to govern humanity. Hwanin granted his son's wish, giving him three heavenly treasures (or seals), and sent him to Earth. Accompanied by a retinue of 3,000 spirits, Prince Hwanung descended to the summit of the Taebaek Mountains, beneath the sacred sandalwood tree. Together with the Earl of Wind and Chancellors Rain and Cloud,

A painting of Dangun, depicting him over Mount Paektu and its crater lake. In ancient times, Paektu was considered the 'head' of the Taebaek Mountain range's 'spine'.

Hwanung supervised all aspects of life, such as agriculture, justice and medicine.

At that time, near the sacred tree, a bear and tiger were living together in a cave. They deeply wished to become human, and every day, at the base of the tree, they asked that Hwanung transform them. Hwanung was moved by their earnest desire. He gave them twenty garlic bulbs and a bundle of mugwort and said to them, 'If you eat these and stay inside your cave for one hundred days, you will become human.'

So the bear and tiger took the garlic and mugwort and went inside their cave, where they fasted for twenty-one days. The tiger wasn't able to continue the fast and left the cave, but the bear endured the hunger and became a beautiful human woman named Ungnyeo (웅녀 / 熊女, 'Bear Woman'). As there was no one she could marry, Ungnyeo again went to the base of the sacred tree every day and asked to have a child. Hwanung himself changed his form and married her. She became pregnant and had a son, Dangun, who would reign as the first human king of the peninsula.

Dangun created a new capital at what is now known as Pyongyang Province (which is located in Manchuria), and gave the kingdom the name Joseon (now known as Gojoseon). Later, he moved this capital city – Asadal – to a mountain, possibly what is now Mount Kuwol. Dangun ruled the nation for 1,500 years, and it is said that when he abdicated the throne to the next king, he became a mountain god.

Pak Hyeokgeose and the Founding of Silla

The *Samguk Yusa* goes on to describe the founding of Silla, referring back to ancient mythic times and supernatural phenomena, such as luminous eggs, that are associated with divine and solar origins.

In the old days, six clans inhabited the area of Seorabeol (서라벌, which is Gyeongju today), and all did as they wished. They were the Yi, Jeong, Son, Choi, Bae and Seol clans, and each of them claimed to be descended from divinity. One day, the ancestors of each clan took their descendants to a hill above the Ai River and held a discussion. They decided they needed a virtuous king to govern the people and found a nation, a king who could protect them from attacks by outsiders.

From the hill, they worshipped and asked for a gracious ruler. Suddenly there was a flash of lightning, and a rainbow touched the ground to the south, at the Na-jong well at the base of Mount Yang

The Heavenly Horse as painted on a birch-bark saddle flap in 5th-century Silla – a Korean national treasure. This artifact was found in Cheonmachong Tomb, Gyeongju.

[what is Namsan, or 'South Mountain', in Seoul today]. There, a white horse stood, and it seemed to be bowing to something. When the people came to the spot, the horse gave a cry and flew up to Heaven. Where the horse had been, the people found a red (some say blue) egg lying on a giant rock by the well.

When they cracked open the egg, a beautiful boy, whose face shone like the sun, hatched from it. The people bathed him in the East Stream. He looked even brighter then, and the people danced with joy. Even the animals sang and danced around him. Heaven and Earth shook, and the sun and moon shone brightly. The people called the boy Hyeokgeose (혁거세 / 赫居世, 'Ruling with a Bright Light') and welcomed him, hoping he would marry a virtuous queen.

On the same day, a dragon descended to another well – Aryeongjeong in Saryang-ni – and from the left side of her ribcage, a baby girl burst out like a flower from a bud. (Some people say the dragon died, and the baby was found inside her body.) The girl was very fair and graceful, but her mouth was like a chick's beak. However, when she was bathed in the north stream of Moon Castle, the beak fell off, revealing human lips.

The people erected a palace at the foot of Mount Yang and raised the two babies, who grew up to be a noble prince and princess. Because Hyeokgeose's egg looked like a gourd, he was named Pak (박), which means 'gourd' (its pronunciation is very close to *balg*, '밝', which means 'bright'). The princess was named Aryeong (알영 / 閼英), after the well where she was born. At age thirteen, the two were crowned king and queen consort. The nation was called Seorabeol (서라벌 / 徐羅伐, meaning 'capital city' and pronounced 'Syerapel' in old Korean), and in later times, was called Silla (신라 / 新羅), signifying a 'New Settlement'.

Hyeokgeose thus founded Silla, and went on to rule for sixty-two years. He then ascended to Heaven, and after seven days, his ashes fell to the earth and scattered. The queen ascended to join him, and her ashes fell to the earth also. The people of the kingdom wept over the ashes and wanted to bury them both in the same tomb, but a great snake appeared and stopped them. So instead, the king and queen's remains were divided into five parts, and separate funerals were held. The Five Mausoleums, or Sanung (사능 / 巳陵, 'Tomb of the Snake'), were built to house the remains. Their son, Crown Prince Namhae, succeeded Hyeokgeose as king.

Cheomseongdae (첨성대 / 瞻星臺, 'star-gazing tower'), located in Gyeongju, as constructed in 7th-century Silla. It is the oldest observatory in Asia and one of the oldest in the world.

Chumo and Goguryeo

The kingdom of Goguryeo came out of Buyeo. One day, the king of Buyeo, Hae Buru (해부루 / 解夫婁), was told by his minister that he had received a divine message in a dream telling him the kingdom should be relocated to a more fertile land. The king did so and renamed the kingdom Eastern Buyeo. However, back in his old territory, a man named Hae Mosu (해모수 / 解慕漱) took the throne, claiming to be of divine ancestry.

One day, King Hae Buru's successor, King Geumwa (금와 / 金蛙 or 金蝸, literally 'gold frog' or 'gold snail'), was travelling south of the Taebaek Mountains. There he met a woman named Yuhwa (유화 / 柳花, 'Willow Flower'), the daughter of Habaek (하백 / 河伯, 'River Lord', said to be a dragon king in certain versions). Yuhwa said that she had encountered Hae Mosu, the man who claimed to be the son of a god, and that he had slept with her near the Yalu River, by Ungsim ('Bear Spirit') Mountain. Because she had had an affair without her escort, Yuhwa's family had exiled her. The king of Buyeo thought this story odd, and confined Yuhwa to a room.

Rays of sunlight beamed into the room. Yuhwa tried to avoid them, but they followed her wherever she went, and when they touched her she became pregnant. (In older versions of this story, a ball of light the size of a hen's egg impregnated her instead.) She soon gave birth to a large egg. The king threw it into a pigsty, hoping the pigs would eat it, but they would not harm it. He threw it to the dogs, horses and cows, and all of the animals avoided it. When the king cast it out into a field, birds came down and shielded it with their wings. The king even tried to break the egg, but it would not break. Eventually, he returned it to its mother, who wrapped it up and kept it warm. A boy hatched out of it.

He was an excellent shot with a bow, and he was given the name Chumo (추모 / 鄒牟). The king and his people distrusted Chumo, and wanted to get rid of him because he was not human, and therefore unnatural. Chumo suspected this, so when he was put in charge of feeding the horses, he gave the better horses less food to make them thin and the poorer horses more food to make them fat. Not realizing this, the king chose one of the fat horses for himself and gave a thin one to Chumo. One day, they went hunting, and Chumo was able to bag far more game than the king because of this trick.

When the king was ready to have Chumo killed, Yuhwa told Chumo to escape. He listened to her and rode off with a few friends, pursued by the people of Buyeo. Chumo and his friends reached a great river with no way to cross. Just as the people were about to catch up to them, Chumo declared, 'I am a divine son and the

A Goguryeo clay roof tile with the face of a stylized beast (possibly a *dokkaebi*), 5th or 6th century CE. Decorative roof tiles have a long history in Korea.

maternal grandson of Habaek. Help me!' At this, fish and turtles rose to the surface of the river and formed a bridge, and Chumo and his friends could cross. The fish and turtles swam away before the pursuers could follow.

Later, Chumo came upon three people, one wearing a cloak of taro, another wearing monk's robes, and a third wearing dried weeds. They joined him, and until they could erect a palace they built a temporary dwelling together beside the Biryu River. Chumo changed his family name to 'Go' (고 / 高), meaning 'high', and because of this, he named the land Goguryeo (고구려 / 高句麗), meaning 'High and Beautiful'.

The Origins of Clans and Other Foundation Myths

There are many other Korean foundation myths, and they tend to share the same primary themes and imagery that run through the myths of Dangun, Hyeokgeose and Chumo. For example, in the story regarding the origin of the Kim clan, purple clouds descend from the heavens surrounding a golden box, and when the box is discovered, a white rooster is crowing beside it. The box opens, and inside is a boy who later takes the name Kim (金), meaning 'Gold' (see p. 158). Here, though one might expect a hen, the presence of a rooster associates the box, which figuratively hatches, with the many eggs that appear in the other foundation myths.

As with the creation myths discussed above, the stories told on Jeju Island differ from those of the mainland. The foundation myth regarding the settlement of Jeju Island features three wise men magically emerging from the ground from a cave on the side of Mount Halla. They marry three women of divine descent who were held inside two boxes, one made of wood and wrapped in purple cloth, and the other made of stone. The women were daughters of kings of Japan, sent across the sea to marry the three leaders of Jeju and bring civilization to the island.

Korea's Mermaids: The Diving Women of Jeju Island

Haenyeo (해녀 / 海女, literally 'sea women') are female free-divers who have been practising their craft on Jeju Island for over 1,500 years. Historically, the men of Jeju engaged in activities like farming and fishing, while the women took on the responsibility of diving for marine resources including abalone, sea cucumber, seaweed, octopus, sea urchin, conch shell and shellfish. It is said that Jeju is the place of 'three lacks' and 'three plenties': there are no thieves, beggars or gates, and there are plenty of rocks, wind and women. Historically,

Haenyeo swimming in the sea. This photo was taken by folklorist Seoknam Song Seok-ha, who spent many years cataloguing Korea's indigenous beliefs.

the proportionally large number of women on the island was due to so many fishermen being lost at sea in the rough waters.

Haenyeo practise traditional free-diving, which means they dive without the use of any breathing equipment and, until the late twentieth century, without wet suits. One legend tells that the Sea Goddess was touched by the hardships faced by Jeju villagers and gifted a group of women the ability to breathe underwater. In another variant of the legend, the first *Haenyeo* was a woman whose husband was lost at sea. The Sea Goddess, moved by her dedication, allowed her to breathe underwater to help her find her husband. It is said that the *Haenyeo*, because of their exceptional diving skills, are the only humans who can visit the underwater palace of the Dragon King on their own and that they age backwards. Some *Haenyeo* are practising shamans, although most of the shamans on Jeju are men (in contrast to the mainland, where most shamans are women).

The *Haenyeo* community is unique: in a culture that is predominantly Confucian, they have maintained a tight-knit matriarchal society in which women hold economic and social power, and mothers teach their daughters the skills and traditions associated with diving. Yet in recent decades, the number of *Haenyeo* has declined due to the arduous nature of the work, the aging population, and changing economic opportunities for women. Efforts are being made to preserve and promote the tradition, and *Haenyeo* are recognized by UNESCO as an Intangible Culture Heritage.

RELIGION IN KOREA

Korea has a rich history of indigenous religious tradition, and has also embraced a number of religions brought to the peninsula via cultural exchange and by missionaries. Korea is notable for the syncretism of its religion and myth: just as shamans use the names of buddhas in their songs, so too will Buddhist temples have shrines to the Old Man of the Mountain, and Christians will participate in Confucian, Buddhist and even Shamanic rituals. This chapter will cover Korea's three earliest religious traditions, animism, Shamanism and Taoism, as well as the imported belief systems of Confucianism, Buddhism and Christianity, and consider the ways in which they blend into each other in modern Korea.

ANIMISM

There is debate regarding how far the earliest kingdoms that could be called 'Korean' or 'proto-Korean' extended into what is now Manchuria and China, and exactly how old these first kingdoms were (the oldest Korean histories are certainly exaggerating at points). What is clear, however, is that the first beliefs of the people of the peninsula and Jeju Island fell under the general rubric of animism. Thus the very first religion 'indigenous' to Korea was animist, characterized by the idea that all living and non-living things have spirits, and that these spirits are accessible to everyone. Korea's cosmological origin myths make this clear with their references to humans being created from animals, animals speaking, ghosts walking the earth, and the anthropomorphizing of natural phenomenon.

In addition to oral and recorded narratives, many different types of material objects reveal the history of Korean animism. For example, thousands of dolmens that date back to Neolithic times are found throughout the peninsula. Entombed alongside the bodies that lie beneath these dolmens are not only items that served clear practical purposes, such as pottery, but also items that suggest

Jade and silver *gogok* from the 6th century CE.

Gold crown from the Silla period with *gogok* as ornaments.

Stereograph of villagers gathered before a row of *jangseung, c.* 1919.

important symbolic meaning, such as *gogok* (곡옥 / 曲玉), which are shaped like cashews. *Gogok* were probably used as jewelry; they have a single hole (which gives them a remarkably fetus-like appearance) and are carved from precious stone – typically a hard stone with a translucent quality. (While many different minerals fall into this category, in Korea, they were all generically referred to as 'jade'.)

In later times, including the Three Kingdoms period, *gogok* were worn by kings and shamans to indicate their association with both political and spiritual power. Since prehistoric times, these carved objects have very closely resembled the *pa* (파 / 巴), the swirling shapes inside the *taegeuk* (see pp. 24–25), and, even more closely, the two halves of the yin-yang symbol. These similarities make it highly likely that *gogok* represented or were intended to tap into a spiritual force, and although their specific function remains a mystery, the trajectory of their usage throughout the ages casts light upon the evolution of Korea's religious traditions.

Jangseung (장승 / 長承) are wooden posts carved and painted with frightening faces and traditional hats. While Westerners, particularly missionaries, often referred to *jangseung* as 'demon posts', these totems were erected around villages to ward off evil spirits and are more properly classified as 'anti-demon' posts. They are usually erected in male and female pairs marked with Chinese characters, which typically read 'Great General Beneath Heaven' on the male post and 'Female General Beneath Earth' on the female post. *Jangseung* were generally created by average people rather than trained artisans and tend not to be carved in a naturalistic style because they are meant to be intimidating.

SHAMANISM

While closely related to animism, Shamanism – also sometimes referred to as Muism, from the word *mu* (巫 / 무) – builds on the fundamental belief that all people have access to the spirits around them. Anthropologists who study religion generally consider Shamanism to be an evolution of animism because it accompanies the development of more complex social organization. Shamanism involves individuals – shamans – who are considered more suited to accessing the spirit world than others. The shaman is able to enter an altered state of consciousness to communicate with or channel spirits in order to help or heal other members of the community.

The tradition of Korean Shamanism is old and vast in its own right, its roots also tracing back to proto-Korea and likely linked to Shamanic practice in the ancient cultures of the Asian steppes. Artifacts clearly belonging to the ruling classes that invoke Shamanic imagery, such as *gogok* and antlered headdresses, indicate that there was a time when shamans held great political power. Korean pseudohistorical documents also speak of a 'golden age' in which shamans ruled as kings and queens. Korean Shamanism was more widely practised at the local level, however; every village or neighbourhood would have had its own shaman who played an important role in local communities, being hired to perform rituals in order to grant blessings or boons (for example, in the name of increasing a farmer's harvest), exorcize and placate spirits, divine sources of misfortune, and even simply to entertain. It is still widely

A 19th-century print by Shin Yun-bok that depicts a dancing shaman.

practised today, even in one of the most wired and technologically advanced countries in the world.

Shamans and their Role

Traditionally, Korean shamans are born female, though on Jeju Island they may be born male. They are chosen by *shinbyeong* (신병 / 神病, 'spirit sickness', usually referred to as 'possession sickness' in English). The signs of *shinbyeong* vary, but include both physical and psychological symptoms, such as hallucinations, insomnia, malnourishment and bodily dysphoria (the feeling of being in the wrong body). *Shinbyeong* can last for years, even into adulthood, and it is believed that the only way to cure it is to become a shaman. In another tradition, the role of shaman is inherited. Shamans who inherit the role, known as *sseseummu* (세습무 / 世襲巫), use a medium to communicate with spirits instead of being possessed themselves. Those who specialize in becoming possessed by spirits are known as *manshin* (만신 / 萬神, literally 'Ten Thousand Spirits').

The most well-known category of Korean Shamanic rituals and rites is the *gut* (굿). In order for *shinbyeong* to be healed, the afflicted must be inducted by an experienced shaman through a *gut* that involves being possessed by spirits. Other *gut* (of which there are many types that developed in different parts of the peninsula) involve bringing boons to individual villages, farms or fishing trips, exorcizing unsettled spirits and ensuring the dead reach the other world safely, and even simply securing an individual's good fortune. A shaman's role essentially involves problem-solving for members of the local community.

As discussed in Chapter 1, the *muga* (무가, 'shamans' song') is another common ritual that appears in various contexts. Shamans

– particularly the shamans of Jeju Island – not only recount the lives of the dead for their families during funerary rites, but also sing the origins of the world and humanity. *Muga* are also used during *gut* for the purposes of exorcism.

Another Korean Shamanic ritual is the *talchum* (탈춤), or mask dance. There are many individual versions of the mask dance across Korea, but generally they involve shamans donning masks designed to represent social archetypes or spirits, such as 'the general', 'the

Shamanism and Gender

Shamanism has long been a way for the oppressed, such as women, transgender people and gay or lesbian people to express and support themselves and their communities. The life of a shaman has historically allowed women – who may otherwise have been outcast due to being widowed or having abusive husbands – to earn money and support themselves and their families. And while Shamanic rituals in Korea often involve cross-dressing, the phenomenon goes even deeper. The symptoms of *shinbyeong* are often characteristic of gender dysphoria, and when embodying a spirit of a different gender, the shaman quite literally *becomes* that gender.

Shamanic rituals also allow for play, and for ridiculing the people traditionally in power in Korean society. Even though Shamanism has faced suppression throughout Korean history by Confucians, Buddhists and Christians, as well as by nearly every political administration in modern times, the fact that it was and continues to be a decentralized religion makes it a powerful tool for the marginalized in society. Even with its role in the corruption scandal that resulted in the arrest and conviction of Park Geun-hye – Korea's eleventh president and daughter of the former dictator Park Chung-hee – in 2017, the Shamanic tradition continues and thrives, and archetypes like the feminine male shaman are common in Korean popular media (see p. 205).

A traditional Korean funeral procession with the bearers carrying
a bier to the mountain for burial, *c.* 1890–1923.

bride', or 'the syphilitic monk'. During the mask dance, each archetype serves a different function, able to grant a different blessing
or type of protection. The mask dance originated as a funerary ritual
to exorcize evil spirits and protect the dead from them, but later
developed as a vessel for entertainment and social commentary
criticism as well. There is a theatrical element to the mask dance
and to many Korean Shamanic rituals.

Channelling Spirits

There are more Shamanic deities than can be counted – they likely
number in the thousands. This is because every village has a shaman,
and every shaman communicates with or channels their own set of
spirits and deities. However, there are certain categories of deities
that are common across Korea. In fact, many of the spirits and

deities Korean shamans channel and communicate with are arche-types based on people found in daily life. This is clear not only in the mask dance, but also in the rest of their rituals.

The Great General Spirit, for example, is one of the main figures channelled by Korean shamans, and is referenced on *jangseung*. The Great General can be a specific general or a conglomeration of generals from throughout Korea's history. The Grandmother Spirit (산천할머니, literally 'Landscape Grandmother') is a folkloric entity who represents an old woman's wit and wisdom; unlike the Great General, she is not based on a specific historical figure, but might be associated with wise old women from an individual shaman's local community.

Mask dance masks depicting two different archetypes: the syphilitic monk and the bride.

Princess Bari and the Origin of Female Shamans

The female shamans of the Korean mainland trace their origins back to the mythic figure of Princess Bari, whose story resonates with the ordeals shamans must endure in their own lives. It is one of the most important examples of a legend that exemplifies female virtue.

Long, long ago, there was a king named Ogu. He was only fourteen when a fortune-teller told him he'd have a fine heir if he married Lady Gildae. So Ogu agreed to marry her, and an astrologer was consulted to pick an auspicious date for the wedding. The king was warned to abide by the Law of Heaven, but he was young and impatient, and he made Gildae his queen one day early.

Misfortune after misfortune fell upon them. The queen bore six daughters in a row. Even though the king's advisors tried to comfort him and said surely the next child would be a son, the king brooded. Meanwhile, the queen had a *taemong* [birth dream] portending that her next child would be an exile from the Heavenly Kingdom, the daughter of an immortal named Seowangmo, guardian of the elixir of life.

When the seventh child was another girl, the king was furious and disowned Gildae, commanding she be cast out to die. Before the eyes of her weeping mother, the infant was sealed in a stone chest that was then taken out to sea and thrown into the deepest part of the ocean.

The chest sank, but how could Heaven allow such cruelty to an innocent? Divine intervention came to the infant's rescue [in various versions of the tale, it's the Dragon King, the Buddha, or even a stork] and the chest floated back up. Eventually, the currents carried it to shore, where it landed at the feet of a kindly old Buddhist monk. He noticed the king's seal on the chest and, thinking it held a great treasure, took it to the local temple to be opened. But to the monks' horror, a baby girl was inside. The monks had all heard the story of the king's seventh daughter, and knew they would be punished for saving her life. But they were holy men and wouldn't let her come to harm, and so the old monk hid her in the temple and raised her as his own. He named her Bari, which was short for Barideggie ('Little Abandoned/Thrown-Away One').

As Bari grew, she showed great intelligence and signs of divine favour. When she was old enough to ask about her parents, the old monk told her, 'Your father is the spirit of bamboo, and your mother is the paulownia.' Bari paid her respects to the spirits of these plants as if they were her ancestors.

One day, a shaman came to the temple, searching for the king's seventh daughter. 'The king is gravely ill,' the shaman said to the monk, 'and he will die unless his missing daughter is found.'

'We fear King Ogu's wrath,' said the monk. 'He commanded his daughter be put to death. How will our temple fare if she's discovered here? How do we know this isn't a ruse to find her and kill her?'

'You need not fear the king now. His six daughters have all failed him, and now he seeks the seventh out of desperation and a change of heart.'

And so it was revealed to Bari that she was the king's daughter, and she returned to the palace to much rejoicing. But the king was still gravely ill – the only way to cure him would be for one of his children to find a medicine in the distant West, in a heavenly land beyond India. [In some versions, both the King and Queen have fallen ill, and both need to be cured.] The king's other daughters had been too afraid to make the long and perilous journey, but Bari agreed.

Donning men's clothing, Bari set off on her quest to Seocheon Seoguk (西天 西國, literally 'West Sky West Country', meaning the Western Paradise). She travelled for thousands of *li*, across wide plains, over high mountains, and fording great rivers. She even journeyed through the underworld, and once she reached her destination, she married a giant and bore him sons in exchange for the medicine to heal her father.

After seven long years, she journeyed back through the underworld, freeing the spirits of the unjustly deceased as she went. When she returned to this world, she cured the king, who forgave her for marrying without his permission.

Bari became the goddess who presides over death rites, which are said to be named *ogu* after her father. Men carry a bamboo pole and women carry a pole cut from a paulownia tree in funeral processions because Princess Bari treated the bamboo and paulownia as her parents. And because Princess Bari was unjustly cast away and endured great trials – journeying through the underworld and communing with the dead – yet remained virtuous, faithful and devoted all the while, the female shamans of Korea trace their lineage back to her.

TAOISM

The oldest of the imported 'non-native' Korean religious traditions is Taoism. As far back as the thirteenth century, the *Samguk Yusa* refers to Chinese Taoist folk hero and deity Fuxi. However, Taoism's history in Korea is far longer than what has been preserved in historical texts that were influenced by Buddhism and Confucianism.

Taoist principles were spread to Korea as early as the Three Kingdoms period, during China's Tang dynasty (618–907 CE). In the seventh century, Taoist philosophers were sent from China to Goguryeo, bringing with them the *Tao Te Ching* (道德經, also Romanized as the *Daodejing*), the foundational text of Taoism.

While Taoism would never become an institutional power in Korea, in the way that Buddhism did, Taoist principles and beliefs were subsumed into the major religious practices, folk religion and daily life. This is why Taoist influence can be seen in such diverse places as Shamanic shrines, Buddhist temples and the Korean flag. Korean Taoism is also unique and distinct from the Taoism that originated in China because elements of folk religion and traditional medicine (both Chinese and Korean) became mixed with Taoist philosophy.

Core Beliefs of Taoism

Taoism (also known as Daoism) is an ancient philosophical and religious tradition that originated in China. The central concept in Taoism is the Tao (도/道 Dao), usually translated as 'The Way', an abstract and ineffable principle that represents the fundamental force or source of everything in the universe: 'The Tao that can be spoken is not the eternal Tao.' It is often described as the natural order of the universe, the way things are meant to be. The Tao is both the process that characterizes everything – the 'is'ness of the entire universe – and also the way or the path to harmony and balance with the universe.

In Taoist cosmology, humans occupy a unique position between Heaven and Earth, and we can harmonize with the Way of Heaven and the Way of Earth by cultivating *qi* (氣), *gi* (기) in Korean, the

---

Fan Death!

One of the most curious contemporary Korean superstitions, which seems to persist despite abundant evidence to the contrary, is the belief that sleeping in a room with a fan blowing can be fatal. Academics and scientists have been puzzled by this head-scratcher for decades, and various theories have been offered: it was a government ploy to keep people from wasting electricity during the post-war years; it was a simple superstition designed to save on electricity bills when electricity was prohibitively expensive; it was a result of ignorant people dying of accidental electrocution. The belief is so prevalent that there's even a Wikipedia entry devoted to it.

The truth behind this superstition is likely to be related to earlier beliefs and practices associated with Korean *qigong*, or Taoist energy cultivation. Of course, both rural and urban Koreans of previous generations knew of the dangers of hypothermia, which is seriously amplified by wind chill. Anyone familiar with the climate of the Korean peninsula will know this. But in the practice of energy cultivation, one of the principles is not to practice with wet feet, in water, or in a significant wind because all of these will strip one's body of *qi*. One's sleeping body is thought to be especially vulnerable, because the spirit is often wandering (perhaps in dreams).

---

life force that permeates the cosmos. By also living in accordance with the principle of *wu wei* (無為; 무위 *muwi* in Korean, usually translated as 'non-action'), instead of the typical human striving for material success and control, we may align with the natural flow of the Tao and achieve longevity and even immortality while avoiding the burden of karma (see p. 80).

Taoism in Korean Culture and Ritual

The seminal text of Taoism is the *Tao Te Ching* ('The Classic of the Way and its Virtue'), written around 400 BCE and attributed to Lao

Tzu (老子, also known as Laozi), a semi-historical figure. The *Tao Te Ching*, with its eighty-one poetic verses divided into two sections, *Tao* and *Te*, is most likely a compilation of the sayings of many old sages and describes the core religious and philosophical principles of Taoism. The *Chuang Tzu* (莊子, also *Zhuangzi*), named for the sage Chang Tzu, is Taoism's other central text. It is more accessible and extensive than the *Tao Te Ching* – which is often cryptic and enigmatic – and features parables, anecdotes and philosophical essays that illustrate the principles of Taoism. These texts, along with the oracular *I Ching* (易經, 'The Book of Changes'), Taoism's third central text, were first brought to Korea in the seventh century by the Chinese.

In both Chinese and Korean Taoist beliefs, there are two main concepts. One is *wuji* (無極), the 'empty ultimate', pronounced *mugeuk* (무극) in Korean. *Mu* is the primordial emptiness from which everything emerges and in which everything can be contained,

---

When Lao Tzu Met Confucius

Because they were likely to have been contemporaries, there are stories about Lao Tzu and the Chinese philosopher Confucius meeting. The most well-known is that Confucius, who usually travelled with his disciples, went alone to meet Lao Tzu and ask him questions about rites. Lao Tzu said, 'You speak of men who have rotted away with their bones. Nothing has survived but their words.' When Confucius returned to his disciples, he said of Lao Tzu: 'Birds fly, fish swim, animals run. I know these things. Running things can be caught in traps, swimming things can be caught in nets, flying things can be shot with arrows. But a dragon riding the clouds into the Heavens – I have no idea how to catch one! Lao Tzu is like a dragon!'

and therefore *mugeuk* could be described as the source of the entire universe.

It is from the *mugeuk* that the fundamental forces of yin (陰) and yang (陽), pronounced *eum* (음) and *yang* (양) in Korean, emerge, and their dynamic interplay is characterized by the *taiji* (太極), the 'supreme ultimate', *taegeuk* (태극) in Korean. As the well-known yin-yang symbol indicates, with its small dot of white and small dot of black, nothing is ever completely one or the other – each quality has, within it, an element of its opposite. *Eum* and *yang* are both complementary and opposing. Everything in the universe is said to contain both elements in differing proportions – the *taegeuk* is the source of the 'Ten Thousand Things' that characterize all of the phenomenal world.

Taoism holds that as a human, one's life is finite. However, by following the Tao with the practice of *wu wei* or 'non-action' – which means harmonizing all of the aforementioned forces – one can extend one's life and gain longevity, even immortality. Taoism encourages living in accordance with one's own true nature and the natural world, and embracing the innate qualities and rhythms of life. Taoism emphasizes simplicity, spontaneity, humility and compassion, as well as detachment from material desires and ambitions, and the way in which each individual follows the Tao is unique to that individual. This philosophy does not lend itself to institutional power, which is likely what contributed to its absorption into Korea's other religious traditions, rather than holding significant centralized power itself.

TAOIST DEITIES

In Chapter 1, we saw how shamans' songs replaced the old names of the protagonists with the names of buddhas. But Mireuk (the Maitreya Buddha) and Seokga (the Shakyamuni Buddha) were not the only deities whose names were used by shamans in this way. The tale about Grandma Mago creating the landscape takes the name of its protagonist from a Taoist immortal, Magu (麻姑, literally 'Hemp Maiden'). Magu was first described in Chinese sources as a young woman with long fingernails like a bird's talons, a Chinese indication of high status. In legends, she often mentions the sea, perhaps inspiring the Korean tradition using her name for the giant mother who shapes the land out of the ocean. She was also associated with caves, and several mountains in China are named after her. Descriptions of Magu/Mago, who is generally associated with longevity, also serve as the inspiration for depictions of female *sanshin* (see p. 107).

There is debate over the meaning of the character for hemp in Magu's name. While Magu legends appear to have served as an inspiration for a common East Asian myth about a different young deity known as the Weaver Girl, suggesting the 'hemp' indicated textiles or weaving, Magu herself in early depictions did not wear woven clothing. Because of this, other scholars believe her name may come from an association with the medicinal properties of hemp, since Taoists often used psychotropic drugs. However, the Korean name Mago, without the Chinese characters to gloss it, is more likely to be associated with words meaning 'high mother', given her role in that shaman song.

The Jade Emperor (옥황상제 / 玉皇上帝, literally 'Jade High Emperor', also known as 천제 / 天帝, 'Heavenly Emperor') is a Taoist deity who occasionally appears in Korean rituals and myths. While he was just one of many Taoist deities at first, over time he was said originally to have been the son of the manifestation of the *wuji* itself. The Jade Emperor then became the ruler of the heavens (a figure who could be called tantamount to God with a capital 'G'). The unique greenish-blue colour of jade has been associated with Heaven for thousands of years in Korea, as it was in China, and this is perhaps one reason the Jade Emperor became a deity with such authority.

The Jade Emperor is sometimes worshipped in Korean Shamanism, and in Korean shaman paintings that serve as icons one might find the Jade Emperor presiding over an orchard of peach trees – peaches being associated with immortality – with the sun and moon together in the sky (a common motif in Taoist-inspired art). While the Jade Emperor does not feature in Korean culture and history to the degree he does in China, this figure is connected to and conflated with the other God-like deities who feature in the Korean *muga*/origin myths, such as Hwanin (see p. 46), though figures like Hwanin predated the stories of the Jade Emperor that were spread from China to Korea.

Jeon Uchi, Korean Taoist Folk Hero

In Korean folk literature, the figure of Jeon Uchi (전우치 / 田禹治), a Taoist wizard and trickster of the Joseon era, provides prime examples of the magical powers Taoists were said to attain. Jeon is described as a master of medicine, divination, geomancy (finding auspicious sites for graves and homes), calligraphy and poetry. In the *Jeon Uchi-jeon* ('The Tale of Jeon Uchi'), a nineteenth-century novel by an unknown author, he is characterized as a figure much

The Chilseong

The Chilseong (칠성 / 七星, 'Seven Stars') is a deity or set of deities introduced to Korea from China via Taoism, and tracing its history demonstrates how syncretic Korea's mythological tradition tends to be. In China, the Chilseong was a Taoist deity that presided over humanity and could grant good fortune. In Korea, the Chilseong, represented by the seven stars of the Big Dipper constellation, were often invoked during Shamanic funerary rites for protection, and in folk traditions. The constellation was worshipped and considered the place to which the spirit would rise to after death. When Buddhism reached Korea, the Chilseong were adapted into a set of seven individual deities, each represented by a bodhisattva, and shrines to this version of the Chilseong can be found in Buddhist temples all across Korea.

The Chilseong motif is still common in Korean art and culture today (for example, spelled 'Chilsung', it remains the most popular soft-drink brand produced in South Korea) and serves as a great example of how each new tradition that developed in Korea paid tribute to and invoked the old.

Painting of the Seven Stars (Chil Sung),
early 19th-century hanging scroll.

like Hong Gildong, another anti-establishment folk hero. In one Joseon-era tale, it is said that when Jeon Uchi had visitors one day, they asked him to do a magic trick, so he ate rice soup for lunch and then blew the grains out of his mouth, whereupon they transformed into little white butterflies that fluttered away towards his garden.

In another Joseon-era story, a friend asks him if he could get one of the peaches of immortality from Heaven. Jeon Uchi answers, 'What's hard about that?' and then asks for hundreds of coils of straw rope. A servant brings them right away. Then, Jeon points to a child and tells him to come over. Jeon throws the straw rope into the sky, and one end soars high into the clouds while the other end remains on the ground. Jeon tells the child, 'On the other end of that rope are many blue peaches. You should gather them and send them down.' Everyone in Jeon's house comes out to crane their necks and watch the child rising higher and higher. A while later, blue peaches begin falling out of the sky, and the people vie with each other for a chance to taste them – they are sweet and clearly not of this world.

But suddenly, drops of blood fall from the sky! Jeon Uchi is scared out of his wits and exclaims, 'We wanted to eat peaches but ended up killing a child!' The guests, suspicious, ask him what has happened. Jeon explains, 'A guard of the mythical peaches must have informed the Highest of the Heavenly Gods of Taoism and killed him.' Just then, an arm falls from the sky, and then the other. Two legs, the rest of the torso and finally the head follow one by one. The guests go pale with fear. Jeon Uchi carefully collects each of the child's disembodied parts, and joins them back together. After a while, the child sits up and runs away. Everybody shares a look, then bursts out laughing.

Stories about Jeon's feats and adventures are so popular that they have been featured in contemporary Korean children's books,

TV shows and films. A fantasy television series called *Jeon Woo-chi* that aired between 2012 and 2013 set its events in a fictional kingdom founded by Hong Gildong. The 2009 film *Jeon U-chi*, marketed in English as *Jeon Woo-chi: The Taoist Wizard* and also known as *Woochi: The Demon Slayer*, turns Jeon into a kind of Taoist trickster superhero whose costume is the attire of a Joseon-era gentleman, complete with a traditional horsehair hat.

BUDDHISM

Buddhism has greatly influenced Korean culture. Originally developed in India around the fifth century BCE, the Buddhism that reached Korea came from China to the kingdoms of Goguryeo and Baekje in the fourth century CE, and was made the state religion of Goguryeo. Then, in the sixth century, it was made the state religion of the kingdom of Silla as well. Over time, it spread across the peninsula, flourishing particularly during the Unified Silla period (668–935). Only in the Joseon dynasty (1392–1910) did its influence begin to wane.

Because Buddhism was introduced to Korea by Chinese monks, it is Mahayana Buddhism, the dominant tradition in China, that was historically practised by Korean people. The Mahayana (or 'The Great Vehicle') tradition emphasizes the role of the bodhisattva, and focuses on an individual's journey to help all other sentient beings attain enlightenment before entering Nirvana oneself. (The other major sect of Buddhism, the older Theravada tradition, focuses on an individual's journey to enlightenment by becoming an *arhat*, or a monastic.)

After waning during the Joseon era, Korean Buddhism had a sharp resurgence in the years following the Korean War (1950–53), becoming Korea's major religion once more. However, in the twenty-first century, Buddhism has been in decline again. According

Wonhyo and the Skull Water

Wonhyo (원효 / 元曉) was a charismatic and controversial seventh-century monk who popularized Buddhist ideas, particularly those associated with Pure Land Buddhism, across the peninsula. One of the best-known Korean Buddhist stories tells the tale of Wonhyo and his friend Uisang, who were travelling to Tang China in order to study Buddhism and bring Buddhist texts back to Korea. But along the way, they were caught in a rain storm. Seeking shelter, they went into what they thought was a cave. That night, Wonhyo was desperately thirsty, and in the dark he reached out and touched what felt like a drinking gourd. From it, he drank cool, refreshing water.

The next morning, Wonhyo and Uisang discovered that the 'cave' was actually a tomb and that they were surrounded by human remains. Wonhyo had actually drunk rainwater out of a human skull. (In some variants of the story, it is said a *dokkaebi* tricked him into it.) Though he was sick at the thought, Wonhyo also realized how easily the mind alters reality, and how perception is therefore illusion. Knowing this, he did not need to travel to China to learn more about Buddhism – he had already had an awakening, and he let Uisang carry on alone.

There are more tales about the work both Buddhist scholars would go on to do. Though he had to leave the priesthood after having an affair with a princess, and often partook in behaviours traditionally not permitted to Buddhists – such as drinking and visiting brothels – Wonhyo went on to become a prolific teacher and commentator, writing more than eighty philosophical texts in an attempt to reconcile various forms of Buddhist thought. Together with Uisang, he developed what is now the dominant Korean school of Mahayana Buddhism.

to Gallup Korea polls, the percentage of Buddhists in Korea fell from 24 per cent in 2004 to 16 per cent in 2021.

Main Principles of Buddhism

Buddhism traces its roots back to Siddhartha Gautama (563–483 BCE), an Indian prince who was deeply troubled by the suffering he saw outside the palace walls. He rejected his royal birthright and left the palace to become a holy man, his sworn mission being to address the fundamental problems of old age, sickness and death – forms

---

Why the Buddha Sits in that Pose

Representations of the Buddha show him in many different poses, and often performing *mudra*s, hand positions that have specific meanings. One of the most prevalent is the *vitarka mudra*, which is the teaching and discussion pose. A folk tale that both Buddhists and Christians find entertaining reveals the meaning of its gestures.

The story goes that Jesus and the Buddha were up in Heaven waiting to be incarnated on the Earth, so they whiled away the time playing chess. To make the game more interesting, they made a bet. The loser would have a choice: pay, or get a noogie on the forehead. Jesus won the first game. Since the Buddha was a mendicant and had no money, he said, 'I will take the noogie.' Jesus whacked him on the middle of the forehead – *smack!* – and that is why the Buddha has the lump there. Then they played another game, and this time, the Buddha won. 'Well,' said the Buddha, 'which do you pick? Will you pay up or take the noogie?' Jesus was just about to answer, but it was his time to be born on Earth, and so he had to leave in a rush. And that is why the Buddha sits with one hand open, to accept money, and the other hand raised with a finger curled, to give the noogie. He is still waiting.

---

of suffering common to all people. Siddhartha Gautama became the Buddha when he achieved enlightenment as he meditated under the Bodhi tree. He is known as the Shakyamuni Buddha because his lineage was of the Shakya clan. Shakyamuni means 'sage of the Shakyas', and it is the source of the Korean term for the Buddha: Seokga.

Because Buddhism was created as a response to Hinduism, which originated in India, the two faiths share certain key concepts, though they were adapted to mean slightly different things in a Buddhist

Buddha in the classic 'Earth-touching' pose. Seokguram Grotto, Bulguksa Temple.

context. Buddhists, like Hindus, believe in *samsara*, the cycle of continuous birth and rebirth that ends only with enlightenment. What keeps people trapped in this cycle through repeated incarnations is the weight of their *karma*. Though karma is commonly understood as the phenomenon of good acts being rewarded and immoral acts being punished, it is actually more of a causal law. Karma means 'action', and the process of karma is a complex causal chain of actions and their consequences that continue into subsequent incarnations. While the burden of karma is avoided in Hinduism by following one's *dharma* – the social and spiritual duties specific to one's caste and station in life – Buddhism rejects the caste system and introduces the idea of a universal Dharma that applies to all individuals equally.

A key concept of Buddhism is *dukka*, a Sanskrit word usually translated as 'suffering'. This is the idea that suffering is inherent to all life – to every being in the universe. Because Buddhists believe in reincarnation (*samsara*), this suffering will continue even between different incarnations of every being. The way out of *dukka* is the process of becoming enlightened or awakened – becoming a buddha – by following the Four Noble Truths and the Eightfold Path.

The Four Noble Truths are presented as a rhetorically coherent argument: there is suffering, suffering has an origin, there is an end to suffering, and the way to end suffering is by following the Eightfold Path. The steps of the Eightfold Path are: right view, right intention/thought, right speech, right action, right livelihood (i.e. work that is not harmful to others), right effort (i.e. maintaining the right reasons and state of mind), right mindfulness and right concentration. All of this is laid out in the teachings of the Buddha, which are collectively called the *Dharma*. It is said that when a

humble, uneducated man asked the Buddha for the simplest explanation of his teachings that even he could comprehend, the Buddha
told him: 'Do good things, don't do bad things, and learn to control
your mind. If you do these things, you are following the Dharma.'

KOREAN BUDDHISM

The type of Buddhism that has been most influential throughout
Korean history is Seon (선 / 禪) Buddhism (*Seon* being derived from
the Chinese *Chan*, which came from the Sanskrit *dyana*, meaning
'meditation'). It is known more commonly throughout the world
by the Japanese pronunciation, Zen. In China, Buddhism and
Taoism – which have a certain mutual affinity in their underlying

The sixth of the 'Ten Oxherding Pictures' or *sipu* (십우), a popular motif
on temple walls, which show a boy's journey towards enlightenment.

philosophies – had merged to form the Chan tradition. This resonated with Koreans and their penchant for syncretism. Seon
Buddhists believe that the practice of meditation is the key to enlightenment, although a scholarly side to Seon also exists, involving the

---

Reincarnation

Shamanism, Taoism, Buddhism and many Confucians share a belief
in reincarnation. The specific process varies according to the tradition,
but generally, reincarnation follows what is described in Buddhism:
forty-nine days after a person's passing, their soul transmigrates to
a new body (usually an infant just being born), and then, eventually,
after a few years, forgets the details of its previous life. (For Western
Buddhists who insist that Buddhists don't believe in the existence
of a soul, this can be quite a conundrum.)

Perhaps the best description of the process of reincarnation in
all of literature can be found in the late seventeenth-century Buddhist
classic *The Nine Cloud Dream* (구운몽 / 九雲夢), a novel written by
Kim Man-jung, who was an advisor to the Joseon-era king Sukjong.
In the novel, a young monk named Hsing-chen, along with a troupe
of eight Taoist fairies, is sent to Hell by a great Buddhist master as
punishment for a lapse in the novice monk's behaviour when, contrary
to his monastic vows, he abused his spiritual powers and flirted with
the eight fairies while intoxicated by wine. When the nine of them arrive
to stand judgment before Yama, king of the underworld, Yama is
confounded by what he believes must have been a bureaucratic error.
Those nine names do not appear in the logbook of the dead! To remedy
the error, for which he might be punished by his own superior, Yama
has the nine immediately sent back into the world to be reincarnated.
Yama's yellow-hatted emissaries hurl them into the dizzying void:

> [...] a great whirlwind arose and carried the eight fairies and the youth
> off into the void, where they were swirled apart and flung into the eight
> directions. Hsing-chen was borne along by the wind, hurled and tossed
> about in endless space until, at last, he seemed to land on solid ground.

---

study of Buddhist scriptures. One major aspect of Seon Buddhism is a focus on the *gongan* (again more popularly known by the Japanese term, *koan*): a paradoxical question, unsolvable by rational means, that is intended to bring students to an awakening.

When the storm calmed, Hsing-chen gathered his wits and [...] he could see a dozen houses with thatched roofs. Several people were gathered there, talking together within his earshot. 'How marvellous it is!' they said. 'The hermit Yang's wife is past her fiftieth year, and yet she is going to have a child! We have been waiting for a long time, but have yet to hear the infant's cry. These are anxious moments.'

Hsing-chen said to himself: 'I will be reborn into the world of humans. I can see that I am only a spirit now, for I have no body. I left it on Lotus Peak. It has been cremated already, and I am so young I have no disciples to recover my relics and keep them safe.'

As these ruminations about the past filled him with grief, one of Yama's emissaries appeared and motioned him over. 'This is the Hsiu-chou township of Huai-nan Province in the empire of T'ang,' he said. 'And here is the home of the hermit Yang, who is your father. This is his wife, Liu, your mother. It is your karma to be reincarnated in this household, so go quickly. Do not miss this auspicious moment!'

Hsing-chen went in at once, and there sat the hermit wearing his reed hat and a coat of rough hempen cloth. He was preparing some sort of medicine on a brazier in front of him, and the fragrance filled the house. From the room in back came the indistinct moaning of someone in pain.

'Go in quickly. Now!' the emissary urged again. When Hsing-chen continued to hesitate, the messenger gave him a hard push from behind.

Hsing-chen fell to the ground and instantly lost consciousness. It seemed that he had been propelled into some great natural cataclysm. 'Help!' he cried. 'Save me!' But the sounds caught in his throat, inarticulate, until they became the cries of an infant.

Primary Deities

The buddhas most often venerated in Korean Buddhism are Seokga (Shakyamuni), Mireuk (Maitreya) and Amida (Amitabha). Seokga is the Shakyamuni Buddha, the historic Buddha who is the originator of the Dharma. Mireuk is considered the buddha of the next age. It is said that he will not appear until the Dharma – all Buddhist

The *Tripitaka Koreana*

The name of the compilation of the Buddhist canon is the *Tripitaka*, Sanskrit for 'Three Baskets'. It consists of the Sutras (written teachings of the Shakyamuni Buddha), the Sastras (commentaries on the Sutras by other masters), and the Vinayas (rules for the Sangha, meaning the Buddhist monastic order). The *Tripitaka Koreana* includes all of these writings, as well as material that is uniquely Korean.

The *Tripitaka Koreana* was first compiled over the course of seventy years in the eleventh century, but this edition was burned by Mongol invaders in 1232. In 1236, even while the invasions continued, the *de facto* ruler of Goryeo, Choe U, created the Office of the *Tripitaka* Compilation (*Daejang Dogam*) in order to recreate it. This version

Woodblocks of the *Tripitaka Koreana*, stored in the specially built hall.

teachings – have disappeared from this world. In Korea, it became very popular to depict Mireuk in the pensive pose, with his fingers touching his cheek as if he is contemplating something. Mireuk is also popular because of his parallel to the second coming of Christ. Amida is the buddha of limitless light, and the primary deity of Pure Land Buddhism, a sect that became very popular in East Asia and

A printed page of the *Tripitaka Koreana*.

of the *Tripitaka Koreana* took monks and artisans fifteen years to complete, and consists of over 80,000 woodblocks (which is why in Korean the *Tripitaka Koreana* is usually called *palman daejanggyeong* [팔만 대장경], meaning the 'Eighty Thousand *Tripitaka*') with a combined total of over 52 million Chinese characters carved into them. Even preparing the birch wood for cutting took years, involving salt-water soaks and drying in the wind. Once completed, the blocks were stored on Ganghwa Island, later moved to Seoul, and finally in 1938 moved to Haeinsa Temple, where buildings designed based on Taoist principles regarding the balance of elements and together named the Tripitaka Hall are dedicated to the storage and preservation of the woodblocks.

Pensive Mireuk (Maitreya) gilt statuette, from the Three Kingdoms Period. Mireuk was popular during this era, especially among the aristocracy.

that many Korean Buddhists continue to practise. The goal of Pure Land Buddhism is to be reborn into Amida's realm in one's next incarnation. It is said that before he became enlightened, the Amida Buddha made a vow that he would establish the Pure Land, a paradise in the west into which everyone who performed good deeds and recited his mantra would be reborn. All those who reincarnate in the Pure Land would have attained a state equivalent to that of a bodhisattva and would be enlightened, attaining Buddhahood in that incarnation.

Another prominent type of Buddhist deity is the bodhisattva (*bosal* in Korean, 보살 / 菩薩). In Sanskrit, *bodhi* means 'awakened' or 'wisdom', and *sattva* means 'a being'. A bodhisattva is a being who has attained a great awakening or is at the verge of enlightenment, but foregoes their entrance into Nirvana. Instead, they have sworn a vow to help all other sentient beings attain enlightenment before they do. Sometimes, Mireuk is said to be a bodhisattva, who will become a buddha in the next age. Bodhisattvas are commonly depicted with special powers that they have been granted to help all beings, and are often shown as attendants to buddhas. For instance, the Amida Buddha is often depicted as part of a triad, with him in the centre and his attendant bodhisattvas Gwanseeum (Avalokiteshvara) and Daeseji (Mahasthamaprapta).

In fact, Gwanseeum, also called Gwaneum, is the most famous bodhisattva in Korean Buddhism, and one of the most important deities in Korean Buddhism in general. The name, in its various orthographies, means 'one who perceives the sounds of suffering'. Avalokiteshvara was originally a male Indian deity and is male in cultures such as Tibet, but the East Asian versions of the figure – the Korean Gwanseeum, Chinese Guanyin and Japanese Kanon – are all female. The Chinese Guanyin and Korean Gwanseeum, however, are sometimes depicted with a long moustache, while the male versions of Avalokiteshvara have no facial hair. In some cultures this deity is referred to in a gender-neutral way, being neither male nor female. It is theorized by some scholars that a conflation with the Christian figure of Mary influenced the change in sex by the time Gwanseeum reached Korea, as both are associated with mercy and the sea (Gwanseeum is known for watching over sailors and fishermen and saving people who are drowning).

KOREAN CONFUCIANISM

While Korea was aware of Confucian thought by the time Taoism and Buddhism had reached the peninsula in the first and fourth centuries, Confucianism did not take hold in Korea in a significant way until the Joseon era in the late thirteenth century. Until that point, Buddhism had been the national philosophy – Confucianism was a major reason for its waning, and Korea is now the most Confucian society in the world.

Korea is a Neo-Confucian society. This means that it was highly receptive to a form of Confucianism that did not date back to Confucius himself, but was instead compiled in the twelfth century by Song-dynasty scholar Zhu Xi into *The Four Books* (四書). Zhu Xi was a harsh critic of Buddhism, and favoured the metaphysical aspects of Confucianism that had developed since its inception. While he was very interested in Taoist works like the *I Ching* and used similar language to describe elements of his philosophy (for example, referring to a 'universal pure mind' that sounds very similar to the Buddhist idea of 'original nature'), Zhu's

A pair of small wedding ducks, *c.* 1980. Wedding ducks are given to newly married couples in Korea to signify faithfulness.

Civil Exam Culture

A key aspect of Korean Neo-Confucian culture, taking root during
the Goryeo and Joseon era, was the civil service exam (called *gwageo*,
과거 / 科擧, in Korean). Based on the Chinese Tang-dynasty ideal
of statesmen to be well-versed in culture and the art of debate, the
civil service exams determined a man's political rank. Special areas
of the palace were designated as study rooms and test-taking spaces.
The exam tested men mainly on composition (both prose and poetry)
and knowledge of classical literature, with proposed political and
military action being secondary to literary learnedness.

The culture of the civil service exam was so central as to become
mythified. Famous Korean historical figures of these eras are often
said to have achieved the highest score on these exams, and been
honoured by the king himself.

Portrait of a successful civil exam candidate.
On his clothing is a *haetae* (see p. 117).

understanding was that all people are born pure and good, but may be tainted by the influence of the material world, leading to impure desires. He wrote that it was through practising Confucian virtues that the mind could be steered back to its proper course.

Filial piety (효 / 孝, *hyo* in Korean) is the bedrock of Korea's Neo-Confucianism, and one of the key concepts that Zhu Xi under-lined in his works. These are rules that are intended to build good character and dictate how people in different relationships to each other should behave. The Five Relationships are as follows: parent and child, ruler and subject, husband and wife, older brother and younger brother, and friend and friend. In each relationship, with the exception of the friend–friend relationship, one person is always above the other in hierarchy.

Parents, rulers, husbands and older brothers are all above their counterparts, and should behave in a just and considerate way. Meanwhile, children, subjects, wives and younger brothers should all assist and serve their counterparts and do what is asked of them. The relationship between friends differs in that there should be cooperation and an understanding that neither is above or below the other. However, if one friend is the other's senior, even by a small margin, the rules for the relationship between the old and young would apply and thus create a hierarchy in that relationship as well. (This is one of the reasons that in Korea, when people meet each other, they will immediately try to establish who is older.) Filial piety means venerating and caring for one's elders, in order to reciprocate what they have done for their children, and deferring to the people who are 'higher' as defined by the Five Relationships.

Strict gender roles are also central to Korean Neo-Confucianism: namely, that men control the outside (*oe*, 외), public-facing aspects of life, whereas women manage the inside (*nae*, 내) domestic aspects of life. While this has never been true in practice, particularly among Koreans of the lower classes (for example, women working in the rice paddies and handling the frenetic market culture), it is an ideal that informed Korean philosophy, and it is reinforced in myth and literature, especially when the traditional Korean upper, ruling *yangban* class is depicted.

Confucianism informs many aspects of Korean life – even corporate structure in Korea has long been based on the societal structures put forward by Confucianism. The mandatory military service for all Korean men also connects itself back to the same ideas that informed the civil service exam culture, positing to instil in men a preparedness for the workforce and a respect for their higher-ups.

Rituals and Hallmarks

There has been much debate regarding whether Confucianism is a religion or a non-religious paradigm for establishing and maintaining social order and hierarchy. Confucianism suppressed the practice of religions like Shamanism and Buddhism. The Confucian idea that men are above women is antithetical to the genderbending and woman-led Shamanic tradition in Korea, especially since being shamans has always been a method for individual women to earn a living. And as mentioned above, Zhu Xi's philosophy was a strong influence on Korean Confucianism, and he was anti-Buddhist. There are generally no Confucian temples or Confucian priests to speak of. However, many of the features of Confucianism that make it appear not to be a religion would also apply to Korean Shamanism, and Confucianism's impact on Korean society is so far-reaching and affects so many aspects of life, including religious aspects, that it belongs in this section.

One of the most prominent Confucian rituals in Korea is setting out offering at shrines to ancestors. The ceremony involving the table setting is known as *jesa* (제사 / 祭祀), and while ancestral rituals have existed in Korea since prehistory, they became formalized via the codification of Confucianism. There are different types of *jesa* that are held at different times and for different types of relatives, and table settings for *jesa* can be very elaborate and involve placing different food items in specific places.

It is a basic assumption in Korea that other Koreans will partake in Confucian traditions, and that even if they are known to be a rebellious person or dismiss Confucianism in general, it is still an expectation that they will honour the principles of filial piety,

An ancestral grave mound with sacrificial altar.

A traditionally set *jesa* table in front of a folding screen.

visit their ancestors graves at the proper times each year, and so on. Koreans are culturally Confucian even if they reject individual aspects of Confucianism – that is, the degree to which it is codified – and Neo-Confucian themes can be identified in practically every Korean myth and folk tale.

Confucianism and Women

Korean Confucianism cannot be separated from its effects on women. Confucian thinking is that women are below men, and that they must work to serve the men in their life, be it their husband, as mentioned in the Five Relationships, or their father before they are married. They are also expected to sacrifice everything for their sons, as can be seen in many Korean folk stories (see p. 139). There is strong pressure for Korean women to marry young, and

Confucians (Literally) Pissing on Women

The two stories below are examples of folk tales that reveal a double standard in Neo-Confucian Korea regarding women. In one, a drunken young scholar staggers out of an inn. He is in such a hurry to relieve himself that he pisses on the roadside, and as he pulls up his pants, he hears a woman's voice: 'I am eternally grateful to you. I died a maiden, and so I was buried here in a flat grave. But now that you have shown me your most precious thing, I can go into the next world fulfilled.' The man was frightened, but it is said that the woman's ghost helped him pass with the highest marks on the civil service exam. In contrast, another folk tale tells of the danger of urinating on a woman's remains if they have not been properly buried. As a young man is pissing on a bone, he asks it, 'Is it cold?' and the bone says, 'It is cold.' He asks it, 'Is it warm?' and it replies, 'It is warm.' The man is terrified and runs off, but the bone keeps chasing him. They reach a wine house and the man tells the bone, 'Would you please wait for me here? I'll get us some rice wine.' He goes in and escapes out the back door. Several years later, at the same wine house, he sees a beautiful woman inside, so he goes in and tells her about his misadventure with the bone. 'Ah! So it was you!' she exclaims, turning into a nine-tailed fox (see p. 109). 'That bone was me! I've been waiting for you all this time!' With that, she gobbles him up. In this story, the woman is a frightening, demonic figure, while in the first story, she is young and grateful for the honour of being urinated upon.

to be educated only in specific fields and not hold power over their male colleagues.

In Korean myth, women who defy these values – who are ambitious, make power plays or disregard proper lineage – are generally vilified. Huibin Jang, the queen of Joseon from 1689 until she was deposed in 1694, is a prime example. She was originally the consort of King Sukjong before being promoted to queen. In Korean literature and folklore, she is cast as a villainess who hired a shaman to curse and kill King Sukjong's virtuous wife, Queen Inhyeon. To rely on Shamanism is particularly antithetical to Confucian values. Queen Jang is also said to have been so angry when the son she bore for King Sukjong wasn't installed as the new rightful heir that she kicked her own son in the testicles and made him infertile, another act in grievous defiance of Confucianism. After being deposed and exiled, Jang was sentenced to death by drinking poison. In more recent times, this has been recast as a sort of heroic or defiant act in addition to the traditional portrayal as a deserved punishment.

CHRISTIANITY

Archaeological evidence suggests that Christianity may have been in Korea in its Nestorian form as early as the eleventh century, but the earliest documented arrival was via Yi Su-gwang, a diplomat and military official who returned from China with Jesuit theological texts in the early seventeenth century. In 1758, Catholicism was officially outlawed by King Yeongjo of Joseon, believing the new ideas to be subversive and a challenge to the authority of the ruling class. It wasn't until the late eighteenth century that Catholicism returned to Korea in earnest, through the efforts of missionaries from France and China. The Korean Catholic Church traces its origins to 1784, when Yi Seung-hun, a *yangban* (member of the aristocrat class), was baptized in Beijing and brought crucifixes, texts and other items back with him to help him spread word of the new religion.

Christianity, Education and Medicine

The development of education and medicine in modern times is intertwined with the history of Christianity in Korea. A prime example is Yonsei University, one of South Korea's most famous and prestigious universities. Yonsei was founded when Severance (formerly *Gwanghyewon*), the oldest Western-style hospital in Korea – which had been founded by Horace Newton Allen, a Protestant medical missionary – merged with a Christian college that had also been founded by missionaries, including Horace Grant Underwood, a Presbyterian. Underwood also happened to be one of those who had contributed to the translation of the Bible into Korean. Ewha Womans University, another of the most prestigious Korean universities and one of the largest women's universities in the world, was founded as a Methodist mission school for girls by Mary F. Scranton, the first representative of the Methodist Woman's Foreign Missionary Society to go to Korea.

The emblem of Ewha Womans University.

Missionaries and Martyrs

The Confucian elite perceived the new teachings as a threat to traditional Korean values, and Yi Seung-hun was beheaded in what is now called the Catholic Persecution of 1801, becoming one of the first Catholic martyrs in Korea. The nineteenth century would witness intense persecution of Catholics. In 1866, nine French priests and 8,000 Korean Catholics were killed. Yet despite this terrible suppression, the faith endured, and the martyrs became a symbol of the church's resilience.

Because Koreans were already culturally familiar with the mystical aspects of Shamanism, charismatic Christian churches and faith leaders were able to adapt elements of Korea's native traditions to the new religion and evangelical Christianity became an especially powerful force. The first Protestant church in Korea was established in 1883 by Lee Soo-jung, who had been baptized in Japan. American missionaries soon arrived in Korea, some of whom would become prominent in the Christian project to educate Koreans, particularly women. In addition to their role in education, Protestant missionaries would play a crucial role in healthcare and social reform, contributing to the modernization of Korean society. The Presbyterian and Methodist missions were particularly influential, establishing schools and hospitals – some of which are still in operation today. Christianity had become such a phenomenon in Korea that by the time the Japanese annexed Korea, the northern city of Pyongyang had come to be known as 'the Jerusalem of the East'.

Missionaries also advocated for social justice, human rights and democratic ideals. Christian influence was evident in the lives of prominent figures such as Kim Chang-jo, an activist who played a crucial role in the March 1st Movement for Korean independence from Japanese rule. In the twentieth century, the crackdown on the Korean independence movement by the Japanese colonial government led to the executions of many Christian missionaries and the censorship of their publications, once again making martyrs out of Christians and forging a connection between their faith and the Korean fight for independence. The fact that lay people could become faith leaders also made Christianity accessible as a religious tradition of the people. The missionaries' message that all were equal in the eyes of God and Jesus Christ made the religion especially appealing to the working class and peasants, as well as to the emerging middle class – and particularly to women, who were traditionally relegated to positions of servitude under Confucian philosophy.

Missionaries have also brought awareness of Korea to the outside world. The Catholic Church in Korea mandated that its followers learn *hangul* and be able to write in it, but in order to educate the new converts, missionaries first had to become familiar with the Korean language. Thus many of the first translators of Korean were missionaries. One prominent figure in the field of Korean translation was James Scarth Gale (1863–1937), a Presbyterian missionary. He was the first person to translate Korean classics, including *The Nine Cloud Dream*, into English. He also translated compilations of folk tales, created several dictionaries of the Korean language and worked on Korean translations of the Bible. His preferred version of the text made it more accessible and laid the foundation for many Koreans to convert to the Christian faith.

After the Korean War (1950–53), the number of Christians grew rapidly in South Korea, as the devastation caused by the conflict and the subsequent economic challenges led many to turn to faith for solace and hope. Churches became vibrant centres of community life, providing not only spiritual guidance but also social and economic support.

Christian missionaries today often cite Korea as the great mission success story, and many Korean Christians are missionaries themselves – in 2007, Korea was the country with the most missionaries working overseas second only to the United States.

CHEONDOGYO, THE WAY OF HEAVEN

Korea closed its borders in the early nineteenth century, but it was impossible for it to remain a 'hermit kingdom' – as it had become popularly known by the end of that century – forever. In 1866, after a massacre of Korean Catholics – including French missionaries – on the orders of the Joseon dynasty, France invaded Ganghwa Island, which is only about 30 kilometres (20 miles) from the capital. The French planned to march on Seoul and destroy it the way the

The symbol of Cheondogyo, showing Taoist influence.

The ten-storey, marble Wongaksa Pagoda in Seoul. The park where it stands was the site of the first mass protest of Koreans against Japanese colonial rule.

British had destroyed the US Capitol during the War of 1812, but the French failed after fierce resistance and had to withdraw. That same year, the American steamship *General Sherman* went aground near Pyongyang while on its mission to forcibly open trade with Korea and was destroyed by Korean fire ships after a four-day battle. In retaliation, the Americans invaded Ganghwa Island in 1871 with a squadron of five ships and 1,200 men. They killed 350 Koreans according to their estimates before leaving, also having failed. In 1876, Korea made a trade agreement with Japan, and in 1882, signed a treaty with the United States. In 1885, not to be outdone, the British Royal Navy took over Geomun Island for two years.

All of these forced incursions by foreign powers only amplified the great social unrest already brewing in Korea. The introduction of *seohak* (서학/西學), or 'Western Learning', exposed the problems of social hierarchy, particularly because Christian missionaries had also brought literacy to the masses. What happened was a simultaneous uprising against local injustice and foreign incursion: the *donghak* (동학/東學), 'Eastern Learning', movement, which emphasized traditional Asian thought in opposition to imported 'Western Learning' (particularly of the scientific kind) while, at the same time, sharply critiquing the social inequality that traditional Neo-Confucian ideology had maintained under the power of the monarchy.

The intention of the Donghak movement, led by Choe Je-u, a charismatic figure, was to reclaim the Mandate of Heaven (천명/天命), a philosophical concept borrowed from the Chinese dynasties regarding the legitimacy of earthly rule; and integral to that purpose was the creation of a syncretic indigenous religion called Cheondogyo (천도교/天道敎), which literally means 'The Religion of the Way of Heaven'. Choe had studied Christianity and Confucianism while working on his father's farm, and he had later spent time in a Buddhist monastery. His teachings emphasized equality, justice and self-reliance, a message that resonated with the common people who were marginalized and oppressed under the hierarchical Confucian society.

By promoting egalitarian values and advocating for social reforms, Cheondogyo became a significant force for social change and political reform. The religion thus played a major role in the Donghak Peasant Revolt of 1894, a bloody uprising that was led by Choe's followers. It is said that the Donghak peasant army worked in the fields during the day and killed their landlords at night, redistributing their land – this is why Cheondogyo is one of the few religions tolerated in North Korea. Although the uprising was ultimately suppressed by a brutal military response, supported by foreign intervention, that is said to have resulted in between 100,000 and 200,000 deaths, it paved the way for subsequent political movements and contributed to the Japanese Annexation and the eventual modernization of Korea.

Cheondogyo incorporates various elements from Confucianism, Buddhism, Shamanism and even Christianity, and its distinct syncretism sets it apart from other religious Korean traditions. Central

---

The Unification Church of Sun Myung Moon

The Unification Church, also known as the Family Federation for World Peace and Unification, was founded by Sun Myung Moon (문선명 / 文鮮明 1920–2012) in 1954. Moon, who was born in North Korea, claimed to have had a mystical vision in which Jesus Christ appeared to him and asked him to complete His unfulfilled mission to establish God's kingdom on Earth. Moon's later purported goal was to lead a global movement for the unification of all religions in the creation of that heavenly kingdom. To Koreans, the use of the term 'unification' strongly evokes the dream of reunifying the peninsula. In the West, the movement's followers are often colloquially referred to as the 'Moonies'.

Moon was a very charismatic leader and, though staunchly anticommunist, made use of much of the same symbolism and rhetoric used by Kim Il-sung (see p. 158). The *hanja* of Moon's name are auspicious: his surname, 文 (Mun), is a name character that can also be read as 'literature' or 'language'. The second character, 鮮, means 'rare', 'fresh' or 'bright', and the third, 明, which is made up of the characters for the sun and moon, means 'bright' or 'brilliant'. Together, they suggest he is a rare and doubly brilliant speaker. But Moon also purposely Romanized his name to

---

to Cheondogyo is the belief in Cheonju, the ultimate deity or God. This monotheism, which is similar to Christianity, also distinguishes it from other East Asian religions. Like Taoism, Cheondogyo emphasizes the harmony between humanity and nature. It acknowledges the interdependence of humans and the natural world and promotes responsible stewardship of the environment (much like Protestantism). This ecological consciousness predates the modern environmental movement and showcases the religion's forward-thinking principles.

place the Sun and the Moon on either side of the Myung, so that his name became a Taoist talisman, an alchemical symbol of the two brightest heavenly bodies signifying enlightenment and divine illumination. That made Moon the embodiment of a guiding light in the same way that Kim Il-sung was the divine light of North Korea.

Moon's *Divine Principle*, the core theological text of the Unification Church, combines ideas and images taken from Christianity, Confucianism and other traditions, and is similar to Cheondogyo in that respect. Yet the Unification Church has also been likened to a cult: it is known for its elaborate mass wedding ceremonies, referred to as 'Blessing Ceremonies', during which thousands of hand-picked couples would be married at once in a large stadium, and it has accumulated vast wealth by exploiting its members. Moon's vehement homophobic rhetoric is also highly controversial.

Moon himself moved to the United States in 1971, and in 1982 was convicted of tax evasion and spent eighteen months in prison. After his death in 2012, his wife took over leadership of the church, but its public presence and activities greatly diminished. More recently, however, the Unification Church has received criticism for its support of Donald Trump and the January 6th Insurrection in the United States.

Cheondogyo also places great importance on the concept of *Haneullim*, literally meaning 'Honored Heaven' or even 'Divine Sky', a term that shares an etymological root with Hananim and Haneunim, Korean names for God. *Haneullim* – the Cheondogyo term – refers to the divine aspect within each individual, resonating with the idea of the Holy Spirit in Catholicism and the Buddhist idea that there is an 'original nature' – Buddha nature – within each individual. This belief in inherent divinity empowers individuals, leading to a focus on self-cultivation and moral conduct. Cheondogyo encourages its followers to lead ethical and virtuous lives, contribute to society and work towards the betterment of humanity – ideals that resonate with Confucian tradition – while its rituals incorporate elements of Catholicism and Shamanism.

Cheondogyo emerged during a transformative period in Korean history and played an instrumental role in challenging the established order. By advocating for social equality, justice and self-reliance, Cheondogyo offered a message of hope and empowerment to the marginalized masses. Its unique blend of religious beliefs and practices, rooted in a monotheistic framework, ecological consciousness and an emphasis on individual divinity, sets it apart from other Korean religions and contributes to its enduring presence in Korean society.

3

GHOSTS, SPIRITS
AND SUPERSTITION

Korea has a complicated relationship with the supernatural. The societal norm in Neo-Confucian Korean culture was to suppress 'superstitious' beliefs, in accordance with the thinking of Neo-Confucianism's founding philosophers. However, when there were issues on an individual scale, the first thing a family would do is consult the local shaman. James Scarth Gale, one of the first missionaries to translate Korean literature and folk tales into English (see p. 98), noted that Koreans – particularly scholars, who were his closest contacts – were hesitant to discuss supernatural matters in public, but held strong beliefs in them privately. It took nearly two decades before Gale was able to read and translate traditional ghost stories. This tension between rejecting and embracing the supernatural persists in Korea today.

Bad Gifts

Koreans avoid giving combs or shoes as gifts. That is because a comb is used to part one's hair and shoes are used for walking away. Such gifts are thought to be inauspicious ones that could end a relationship. If such a gift is unavoidable, the recipient must pay the giver a token amount of money to neutralize the symbolism. On the other hand, if a Korean gives a wallet, a purse or a bag as a gift, they always remember to include some money in it.

SUPERNATURAL BEINGS

The Korean world is shared with spirits. Some encompass aspects of nature, such as the *sanshin* (산신 / 山神, literally 'Mountain Spirit' or 'Mountain God'), also often called the Old Man of the Mountain, a figure and set of figures now revered by Koreans of all religious denominations. When the mythical king Dangun was said to have retired and become a mountain god (see p. 47), he became a *sanshin*.

The entire Korean peninsula is full of mountains that have long been deemed sacred by the local people, and every significant mountain has a *sanshin*. These are depicted as old, bearded men, often accompanied by a tiger and human-like attendants. Sometimes a

A painting of a male *sanshin* with a tiger.

A statue of a female *sanshin* from Mount Jirisan.

sanshin is shown holding an object that reflects their age and wisdom, such as a walking stick or a calligraphy brush. Erecting a stele carved with Chinese characters in order to represent and venerate a mountain's *sanshin* is an old Korean tradition, but now shrines dedicated to *sanshin* typically feature a painting. Female *sanshin* are rare, but are occasionally venerated, sometimes depicted similarly to images of female Taoist immortals (see p. 72). While there are specific local *sanshin* for every sacred mountain, the Old Man of the Mountain is also an archetype and can function as a single unified deity.

Korean myth is also populated by spirits who became ghosts after being wronged. In Korea, a ghost, or spirit that is not at rest, is known as a *gwishin* (귀신 / 鬼神), meaning 'terrible spirit' or, literally, 'ghost spirit'. A *gwishin* can be created when a person dies and is not at peace, or when someone does something improper to an object and that object then comes to life as a spirit. An example of the latter is the broom ghost, which is created when a broom is contaminated by menstrual blood. *Gwishin* are not necessarily evil, though they can be. Rather, they are by default unhappy, and will disappear if they can be put to rest. The same is not true for *magwi/mamul* (마귀 / 魔鬼 or 마물 / 魔物), meaning 'evil spirit' and often used to refer to a demon.

One well-known *gwishin* is the egg ghost, or *dalgyal gwishin* (달걀귀신). Normally, when viewed from behind, this figure looks like a pale-skinned woman with long hair, but it has a completely featureless face that resembles an egg. Rarely does the egg ghost take much action in urban legend – generally, the entire tale goes that a man is walking at night, sees a woman crying and when he

---

The *sanshin* vs the *samshin*

The similar-sounding *samshin* (삼신 / 三神, 'Three Spirits') differ from the *sanshin*. The *samshin* usually appears as a set of three grandmother deities who protect babies. Occasionally she is also depicted as a single deity named Samshin Halmeoni ('Three Spirits Grandmother'). It was often said that babies were safe from disease and accidents until the age of three because Samshin Halmeoni watched over them.

Rice is often set out as an offering to the *samshin*, either in a bowl or inside a bag made out of a belt tied up into a knot. While they differ from *sanshin*, the *samshin* may influence depictions of female *sanshin*. For example, there is a mountain peak in Korea called 'Samshin-bong', named after the *samshin*.

---

goes to comfort her, she turns around and he is terrified by the egg-like face. It may come as a surprise, then, that the egg ghost is considered a truly terrifying entity. Its reputation may stem from the way in which this story is generally performed with dramatic gestures – complete with dramatic reveal of the missing face – to impressionable young children.

In some variants of the story of the Buddhist monk Wonhyo (p. 77), he is said to have been tricked into drinking from the human skull by a *dokkaebi* (도깨비), a creature often referred to as a Korean goblin. *Dokkaebi* are humanlike beings who have a frightening appearance and supernatural powers. In folk tales they are often known for their trickery, as well as for challenging people who come across them to tests of strength, such as wrestling matches. They will often possess magical items, such as a club that grants wishes when they hit the ground with it, or a hat that turns them invisible.

Dokkaebi speak like humans and are usually found in dark and dangerous places, like caves or dilapidated shacks. Despite being superficially frightening and powerful, *dokkaebi* are usually depicted as having easily exploitable weaknesses, and are also often gullible – in folk tales they are tricked as often as they trick others. Stories of *dokkaebi* are part of the long Korean folkloric tradition of valuing cleverness and the ability to outsmart powerful people and entities. *Dokkaebi* are also not described as being evil, despite often being violent or mischievous, and sometimes they grant people boons.

The *gumiho* (구미호 / 九尾狐, literally 'nine-tailed fox') is a fox demon that can grow up to nine tails, and feeds on people and their souls. The more souls they consume, the more tails they grow. Fox

Beware the Red Hand!

For Korean school children, one of the best known and most terrifying stories is the one about the red hand, particularly because it is so close to their daily experience. It's a story that has many variants, but the key to its scare is in its performance. Typically, the story is about a boy who has to go to the outhouse at night – already a scary thing for children, who tend to be afraid of the dark. After the boy has relieved himself and realizes that he has forgotten to bring toilet paper, he hears a voice from below asking, 'Would you like white paper or black paper?' Of course, the boy is terrified. In some versions of the story, the boy is spared if he chooses the right paper, and only has to endure the horror of a red hand emerging from below to wipe his bottom. If he chooses the wrong paper, the hand grabs him and drags him down into the tank, where he drowns.

In some versions of the story, the boy manages to escape, but the following night, he has to go to the outhouse again. This time he takes a knife, and when the red hand emerges he chops it off and runs away. The next day, the boy notices a fellow student at school with dark circles under his eyes holding his arm in a funny way. When the boy asks what's wrong, the other student lunges forward, showing a bloody stump, shouting, 'You chopped off my hand!' At this point in the story, the storyteller leaps at the audience, performing the old version of the cinematic jump scare.

Well into the late twentieth century, Korean public schools lacked flush toilets and had toilet stalls with tanks below, which made the possibility of the red hand more real. Even into the 1980s, many homes, particularly in small towns and rural areas, had outhouses that were emptied out periodically by 'honey wagons' that would process the waste for use as fertilizer in agricultural fields. But even today, with flush toilets, the story has endured. In contemporary times, with unisex public toilets, there is a more realistically frightening story based on actual news reports: hidden spy cameras in toilet stalls that livestream to the internet.

demons are nearly always female, and disguise themselves as human women, often in order to give men a deadly kiss – though in a few folk tales *gumiho* are the reincarnations of human women who were wronged and prey on the innocent in an attempt to return to human form. It is said that if they consume enough souls (or human livers), they become human.

In some stories, the fox demons can shapeshift at will, while in others they must take something from a human woman in order to do so. In one folk tale about a salt seller who faces off with a *gumiho*, the fox wears a human skull on its head in order to shapeshift; in another story, a *gumiho* uses a stolen dress to transform into a young

A *dokkaebi* doll holding a magic club.

A contemporary interpretation of a *gumiho* from *Hometown of Legends*, a series of horror dramas that aired on the Korean Broadcasting System in 2008.

woman. While fox demons exist throughout East Asia, a unique element of the Korean version is their special orb called a fox marble or bead (*yeouguseul*, 여우구슬). This orb holds the souls of the *gumiho*'s victims and grants the demon their power.

Foxes are not the only evil female demons in Korean folklore; a folk tale with very similar themes involves a Eurasian lynx demon who takes the form of a man's wife at night. To tell them apart, the man holds his wife's hand tightly all night and refuses to let go until dawn – when the demon is forced to transform back into a lynx.

THE KOREAN DRAGON

As indicated by the way it has woven itself throughout the chapters of this book, the dragon (*yong*, 용 / 龍) is one of the key creatures of Korean myth. Depictions of dragons, appearing frequently in Buddhist temples and royal palaces, were often created to ward off evil spirits, and dragons can be found throughout the peninsula in place names, in architectural details like spouts and roof ridges, and in great works of art and literature. In the Joseon era, King Sejong, who ordered the creation of the *hangul* alphabet (see p. 15), commissioned the *Yongbieocheonga* (용비어천가 / 龍飛御天歌, 'Song of Dragons Flying to Heaven'), an epic poetic work that tied the mythic founding of Korea to a lineage of dragons in order to validate the nation's authority.

The Korean dragon shares many traits with the dragon as it developed in Chinese myth, and Korean myth emphasizes the spiritual might of the dragon. It is a chimera, and the animals whose traits it shares are associated in folklore with longevity, wisdom and power: it has the head of a camel, the body of a snake (or sometimes the body of an iguana), the talons of an eagle and the whiskers of a carp. The dragon is also the epitome of *yang* or masculine energy (see p. 71). The dragon's element is wood, but 'wood' and 'wind' are the same element in Taoist tradition, and it is wind that the dragon embodies. It is also associated with the colour blue/green, like jade, and with water. In Korean myth, the Dragon King lives in an underwater palace, and every significant body of water is said to house a dragon or dragon-king of its own. Dragon fire can burn on and in water, but is said to be extinguished by normal fire, and when dragons battle, a thunderstorm results, therefore associating them with lightning. When searching for auspicious sites to build upon, Korean geomancers would describe the energy running through the landscape as dragons. In Korean art, dragons are often surrounded and obscured by clouds, underscoring the fact that they always exist partially in the supernatural plane and not just in our own mundane world.

The dragon can fly without wings due to the bump on its head, called a *cheokmok* in Korean (척목 / 尺木), and is often depicted with a pearl that contains great *yang* (a bit like a positive version of the *gumiho*'s fox marble). Dragons also have nine-times-nine scales, because nine is the number associated with *yang*, but thirty-six of those scales are reversed 'evil' scales associated with *yin*, indicating that dragons are not always benevolent. In Korean myth, however, they are almost always presented as benevolent, though they

A celadon ewer shaped like a dragon-turtle.

Evolution of a Dragon

Folk tales that feature dragons as a central subject often revolve around the desire of other creatures to evolve into them, usually by undertaking a trial to prove their worth. In one such story, a naïve young scholar is manipulated by a boar and snake who have been locked in competition for a thousand years over which will become a dragon. The scholar's kindness towards the snake allows her to ascend, and she blesses him and his family. In a similar tale, a centipede and snake are locked in the same type of competition, but it is the centipede who is shown generosity and ascends to bless the scholar. (This latter story is a rare one featuring a benevolent centipede. Normally, in East Asian myth, centipedes are malicious, and presented as a dragon's foe and evil counterpart. The Korean centipede and snake story may be a variation of the boar and snake story that was influenced by Christianization, meaning the snake was demonized.)

Fish, especially carp, are particularly linked to, and keen to evolve into, dragons. One Korean folk tale involves a sardine who has a dragon dream (an auspicious, prophetic dream). The sardine goes to have it interpreted by a jealous flounder, who purposely gives it a negative interpretation. When the sardine realizes that it has been tricked, it slaps the flounder, which is said to be why flounders have both eyes on one side of the body.

tend to be peripheral figures in folk tales and legends rather than main characters.

In Korean folklore, it is said that when an animal lives a very long time, completes a certain trial or gains enough wisdom, it will gain the traits of a dragon, such as scales or a dragon's countenance. These chimeras are known as dragon-animals and often appear in Korean artwork. Perhaps due to their reptilian nature and being associated with wisdom, long life and the creation of the *I Ching* (Fuxi, Taoist deity and mythical creator of the *I Ching*, is half-serpent), the most commonly seen dragon-animal is the dragon-turtle.

Another common example of a dragon-animal is one that originated in Chinese Chan Buddhism (p. 81) and made its way to Korea: the wooden fish, an instrument used in Buddhist temples. It is a woodblock shaped like a fish with dragon features that can be struck with a mallet to maintain rhythm during chants. In Pure Land Buddhism, it is struck when chanting the name of the Amida Buddha. The wooden fish was adapted into two forms in Korea. The original, small version that could fit in the palm of one's hand is called a *moktak* (목탁 / 木鐸), and a large version that more closely resembles a dragon and is usually suspended from the ceiling is called a *mogeo* (목어 / 木魚). The *mogeo* is usually struck with two sticks instead of a single mallet. The wooden fish are said not to need

A *mogeo* at Buseoksa Temple.

Haetae statue outside of the Seoul royal palace gate.

sleep, and this fits with one of their functions, in which they are used to call monks to attention.

Other mythical composite creatures include the *haetae*, a four-legged animal that looks somewhat like a maned lion, but with dragon scales and horns. It is said to embody justice, and judges whether people are good or evil. It is also said to protect against fires. *Haetae* are very similar to the mythical fu dogs of China or the snow lions of Tibet, and, like those, *haetae* are often depicted in pairs, with statues of them flanking the entrances of temples and other important buildings as guardians. They also lend their name to the oldest ice-cream brand in South Korea.

The *girin* (기린 / 麒麟) is a mythical creature with the body and head of a deer or horse, with horns, scales on its back and the tail of an ox. The term *girin* is also the modern Korean word for a giraffe, because the *girin* was originally a creature in Chinese myth that became conflated with the giraffe during the Ming dynasty. *Girin* are associated with fire, healing and royalty, and in Korean myth they were venerated in much the same way as phoenixes. *Girin* are often depicted on Korean rank badges and royal regalia, and King Chumo of Goguryeo (see p. 51) is said to have ridden one.

The phoenix tends to be associated with kings and emperors, and was often paired and paralleled with the dragon. Like the *girin*, it is a

A celadon incense burner with a *girin* on its lid, probably used in official palace rites during the Goryeo dynasty.

symbol of eternity and rebirth, often appearing in funerary art, and seems to have come from China: the *fènghuáng* (*bonghwang* [봉황] in Korean). In Chinese myth, the phoenix is a chimera of many different birds; colourful pheasant species are especially associated with it. In Korea, this creature and its many rainbow colours came to be associated with peafowl and Buddhism. In Buddhist myth, the 'eyes' on the tail of a peacock are sometimes said to represent the stars in the heavens, or the watchful, ever-present eyes of the Buddha, and the peahen is sometimes said to be the Buddha's grandmother.

A gilt hairpin in the shape of a phoenix, from the Goryeo dynasty.

THE TIGER

Though the Siberian, or Amur, tiger that used to range throughout Korea has long been extirpated from the peninsula (they possibly only rarely visit the mountains of North Korea), it remains Korea's national animal and holds great symbolic value. On both occasions when South Korea hosted the Olympic Games (the Summer Games in 1988 and the Winter Games in 2018), a tiger was the mascot. Tigers appear in Korea's earliest myths (such as the story of Dangun, see p. 46), and came to represent power, wisdom and superiority. Paintings of tigers were used to ward off evil spirits, and Korean storytellers often began their tales with the opening line, 'In the old, old days when tigers smoked tobacco pipes…'.

However, despite representing traits such as power and wisdom – for instance, being included in most of the depictions of *sanshin*, the wise old men of the mountains (p. 106) – tigers in many popular folk tales are gullible figures who get outwitted by a weaker figure. One such example is 'The Rabbit's Judgment'. In this story, a tiger who is trapped in a pit cries for help and a man saves him, but only under the condition that he won't be eaten when the tiger is freed. When the tiger tries to eat him anyway, the man begs it to ask various other characters to determine if that would be fair – a pine tree, an ox and a rabbit. The tree and ox both say that the tiger should eat the man, because humans exploit them, but the rabbit says it can't judge the situation until it sees how the disagreement began, tricking the tiger back into the pit. The rabbit then concludes that there would have been no disagreement if the man had never freed the tiger in the first place, and that 'No one, not even a man, should be punished for kindness.'

Another well-known folk tale about a predatory tiger ultimately being outwitted is 'The Tiger and Persimmon'. In this story, a tiger comes down from the mountains and hears a baby crying. He looks into the window of a house and sees the baby's mother trying to get it to stop crying by naming scary animals, warning it that the noise would attract predators – 'Look, a fox! Look, a bear! Look! The big tiger from the mountain is here, right outside the window!' – but that doesn't stop her baby from crying. The tiger is given pause at how fearless the child must be, but resolves to eat it anyway. Just then, the mother says, 'Look, a dried persimmon!' and the baby abruptly stops crying. The tiger assumes a persimmon must be the most frightening monster of all, and flees (though the listener knows that a dried persimmon is a sweet treat).

A tiger's defeat is even said to have led to the creation of the sun and moon in another famous folk tale. In that story, a tiger kills an old woman who is taking care of two children, a girl and a boy. The tiger then tries to kill and eat them as well, but with trickery they manage to escape to Heaven while he crashes down and dies. (The boy became the sun and the girl became the moon, but eventually she was too modest to enjoy having so many people look at her, so they switched roles so she would be too bright for people to gaze at.) What is the appeal of outsmarting the tiger? It reflects the desire of the common people – the downtrodden and oppressed – to resist those who are in power. Ordinary people had to rely on cleverness in the face of a threat like a tiger, literal or figurative. As recently as the Japanese colonial era (1910–45), rural Koreans were killed and eaten by roaming tigers, though such incidents were rare. In rural villages, it was customary for someone who was followed home by a tiger to loudly announce the arrival of a guest upon reaching the

Korea's National Animal

The decision to crown the tiger Korea's national animal was not a unanimous one. The dragon was considered too strongly associated with China to be a contender for the role, but many Koreans preferred the rabbit, one argument being that the peninsula is shaped like a rabbit facing west. The counterargument is that the peninsula is shaped like a tiger, with the northeastern extension representing the tail. But then again, one of the most popular folk tales about a tiger, 'The Rabbit's Judgment', is about a tiger being outwitted by a rabbit. While the tiger, as a symbol of authority and power, was ultimately chosen, the rabbit remains a popular trickster figure and perhaps better represents the ordinary people of Korea.

Joseon-era painting of a tiger by Seok San.

village. Everyone knew this was code for 'a tiger has come to visit'. That way, someone could send a dog out for the tiger to eat while all the humans escaped into their houses. Koreans knew that tigers were powerful and threatening, and that associated them with royal and colonial authorities, making stories about their defeat all the more gratifying.

Not all tigers in Korean folk tales are duplicitous and gullible; they can also be capable of gratitude and honour. In one story, after a man helps a tiger who has a snake coiled around its waist, the tiger later saves the man from a different snake in return, then brings the man a little dog as a gift. The man raises the dog and it has puppies. One day, the dogs all start barking and the man takes it as a bad omen, so he moves to a different house. Later, he returns to his old house and sees it is full of snakes that had come to take revenge upon him – the tiger had given him the dog as a way to warn him. In another folk tale, a monk saves a tiger that has a bone caught in its throat, and the tiger brings him a mayor's daughter. When the monk escorts her back to her father's house, the mayor decides his daughter and the monk should be married (though the monk and the woman – who becomes a nun – end up living more like brother and sister than husband and wife).

THE WOLF

While there are wolves in the northern part of the Korean peninsula, they do not generally appear in folk tales. There are variants of the story of the sun and moon in which it is a wolf and not a tiger that tries to eat the children, and sometimes wolves are said to have the ability to shapeshift into human form, like the *gumiho*, but most references to wolves in current Korean storytelling are in fact borrowed from the West, like 'Little Red Riding Hood' or 'The Boy Who Cried Wolf'.

In modern Korean literature, one of the most prominent representations of wolves appears in a politically charged short story by Hwang Sun-won (1915–2000), one of the most renowned writers to emerge from the Japanese colonial era. 'Even Wolves' (이리도),

Do Koreans Eat Dogs?

Archaeological evidence shows that Koreans were probably eating dog meat as early as the Neolithic era (8000–2000 BCE), although they were also likely to be companion animals at that time. During the Silla and Goryeo periods, which together extended from 57 BCE to 1392 CE, the consumption of dog was probably not a significant practice, since those dynasties had Buddhism as their state religion, meaning that the consumption of meat in general was discouraged. It is most likely that the practice began to grow during the Joseon era (1392–1897), when Confucians were influenced by Chinese beliefs about medicinal foods.

Dog meat is thought to enhance a person's masculine energy (*yang*), and in the modern era was generally eaten in the form of *bosintang* (보신탕 / 補身湯, literally 'self-nurturing soup'). Eating *bosintang* was especially popular during the three hottest days of summer. (Coincidentally, the hottest days of summer, when Sirius, the 'Dog Star', is prominent in the sky, are called the 'Dog Days' in the West). Since the cultivation of *yang* also contributes to bodily heat and virility, dog meat was also eaten in the winter months and as an aphrodisiac.

Dog meat consumption began to sharply decline after international protests called to ban the 1988 Summer Olympics in Seoul. A 2022 South Korean government ministry report found that more than half a million dogs were consumed that year, although 85.5 per cent of those responding to a survey said they did not eat dog. South Korea passed legislation in early 2024 that bans both the sale and distribution of dog meat, to take effect in 2027. The three-year grace period is designed to permit 'dog farmers' to find other means of supporting their livelihood.

published in 1950 but written while Korea was under Japanese rule, is a story within a story, related by the narrator as he reminisces about his friend's uncle. The uncle describes a time when he was in Mongolia, and tells a story told to him and a Japanese guest by a Mongolian innkeeper. It is a cautionary tale about how three Japanese soldiers were killed by a pack of wolves because they had shot directly at them. The innkeeper explains how wolves will be scared away if one shoots into the air, but will attack relentlessly out of vengeance if they smell blood. When they hear wolves outside that night, the drunken Japanese guest pulls out a pistol and, bragging about how good a shot he is, goes out to scare the wolves away, ignoring the innkeepers' repeated warnings – they're coming from a Mongolian, whom he considers subhuman, after all. He goes out into the night. Shots are heard, along with crying sounds and, later, a scream. The Korean and Mongolian go out to help him, but the Japanese man has disappeared. The following morning, the Mongolian shows the Korean all that he found left of the Japanese man – his pistol, covered in gouges and scratches from the wolves' attempts to destroy the thing responsible for their comrade's death. The story concludes with the Korean's statement, reflecting the title: '*Iri do*', suggesting that even wolves are vengeful, making an implicit parallel to Koreans' and Mongolians' attitudes towards Japanese oppression.

In wordplay characteristic of his training as a poet, Hwang has also layered the title with a range of potential readings. *Iri do* can be read as 'in this way', 'to this extent', and 'the way of wolves'. It is also no coincidence that the first syllable, 'I', is written in *hangul* just like the surname Yi – an allusion to the Yi dynasty, whose rule the Japanese toppled when they took over Korea in 1910. It is doubled, the 'I' and 'Ri' symbols representing the two different ways the surname would be written in the south and north of the Korean peninsula. The story ends up being both descriptive and prescriptive, a subversive political statement about unified resistance, but one whose rhetoric could plausibly be denied in the face of Japanese censors.

RABBITS

As detailed in folk tales such as 'The Rabbit's Judgment' and 'The Rabbit's Liver', rabbits are admired for their cleverness despite their small size. The rabbit came to be representative of the Korean people and Korea's struggle as a smaller nation over which major world powers vied for control. Rabbits have many other symbolic and mythical meanings as well. For example, they are associated heavily with the moon. It was believed, from the time of Goguryeo and beyond, that rabbits lived on the moon and were spirits of the moon itself. Koreans took the Chinese myth of moon goddess Chang'e (called Hanga in Korean) and her pet rabbit – who uses a mortar and pestle to pound herbal medicine – and adapted it in their own mythology. In Korean depictions, the rabbit is shown beneath a laurel/cinnamon tree, whose bark has long been used for medicinal purposes. The lullaby 'Half Moon' (반달, romanized as *Bandal*), which every Korean knows from childhood, is about a rabbit sailing across the Milky Way in a half-moon boat with a cinnamon tree

An embroidery frame for pillow making that depicts a moon rabbit.

A painting by Joseon
court official Cho Tai
Eok depicting rabbits in
moonlight, 18th century.

Ten Symbols of Longevity

In Korean art and culture, there are ten motifs from the natural world that represent longevity. While many of these were already symbols of long life or immortality in Taoist China, in Korean artwork they usually appear together, and they were a popular subject for court painters, particularly in the Joseon era. The symbols are: the sun, clouds, mountains (or rocks), water, pine trees, turtles, deer, cranes, peaches (i.e., the peaches of immortality), and a mythical mushroom species said to grant eternal life. The symbols are all based on the idea of endurance and cyclical return and are usually interrelated. For example, it is said that deer will find the mushrooms, and the clouds are often painted in a way that resembles the shape of the fungus. Occasionally, additional symbols like the moon are added – typically, the red sun rising over the mountains will be balanced by a white moon on the other side of the composition.

A 19th-century painting depicting the ten symbols of longevity.

instead of a mast. Although the rabbit is so strongly associated with the moon, as one of the animals in the Eastern Zodiac it represents the East, where the sun rises, and represents dawn, beginnings and the start of the agricultural year. The rabbit has also been used as a symbol of conjugal prosperity.

MYSTICAL PLANTS

South Korea's national flower is the *Hibiscus syriacus*, also known as rose mallow and in Korean called *mugunghwa* (무궁화 / 無窮花). The etymology of its name in Korean is multifaceted. *Mugung* can mean 'eternity' or 'infinity', and *mu* on its own sounds like the primordial emptiness in Taoism (see p. 70). *Hwa* is generally glossed to mean 'flower', but it also sounds like 'fire'.

In crowns, earrings and other jewelry, particularly from the Silla era, aspen leaves inspired gold ornamentation in Korea. Aspen

Gold aspen leaf earrings from the Silla era.

Food Fables

Why Koreans Eat Onions

In ancient times, so it was said, Koreans were cannibals: people would spontaneously turn into cows, and then be slaughtered and eaten by other people. One man was terrified of this fate, and so he left to go to another place. On his journeys he met a leper, and the leper told him that if he ate onions, he would remain in human form. The man decided to return, but on his way he turned into a cow and was captured by his friends, who planned to eat him. Fortunately, a girl happened to be passing by with onions, and the cow ate the onions and turned back into a man. His friends were surprised and shocked: they had nearly eaten him! They, too, ate onions in order to stay in human form, and that is why, ever since then, Koreans have eaten onions.

Why Koreans Eat Red Peppers

Before the Imjin War, the Hideyoshi invasion of Korea in the late sixteenth century, the Japanese cleverly planted red peppers all over the peninsula. The Japanese looked down on Koreans as 'garlic eaters'; there's even a Japanese saying that goes 'Knock a Korean down and when he gets up he'll have five edible plants in his hands.' They were hoping that the Koreans would eat the red peppers and die, making their invasion easier. But they had made a terrible miscalculation – Koreans loved the hot red peppers. They used it to spice everything, and it became one of Korea's staple foods!

A woman drying peppers in front of a traditional, Korean-style house.

leaves were associated with shamans' dances due to the way they quake and shiver on the branch, echoing that shaking that indicates a spirit is inhabiting the shaman during their rituals. The golden aspen leaves that decorate Silla crowns are so delicate that they often move as if they are in a breeze even inside glass display cases.

Korean ginseng is another plant that has been mythologized across the peninsula. While ginseng does have medicinal properties, it has also been said to be a panacea capable of remedying all ills. Ginseng roots that resemble the human figure are thought to be particularly potent. Korean ginseng hunters, *simmani* (심마니), who search for wild, uncultivated ginseng – believed to be far more potent than farmed ginseng – undergo purification rituals and offer sacrifices to be able to see the 'spirit' of the ginseng. Even in relatively recent times, an anthropomorphic specimen of wild ginseng might be worth a fortune.

A shaman painting of the Sancheon Grandmother spirit holding ginseng.

4

CENTRAL THEMES IN FOLKLORE
AND LEGEND

Korea has a rich oral storytelling tradition. Even though radio, then film and television, and finally the internet have supplanted old modes of storytelling, the image of a grandfather or grandmother sitting on the floor, smoking a pipe and recounting local legends still remains in the popular consciousness. The Korean equivalent of 'Once upon a time' is 'In the old, old days when tigers smoked tobacco pipes'. One folk tale, 'The Story Spirits', even provides a cautionary lesson for the origin of the storytelling tradition: if you hoard stories but don't set them free by sharing them, they may eventually conspire to kill you! This chapter illustrates some major themes in Korean folk tales – namely cleverness, female virtue and sacrifice.

CLEVERNESS

Throughout Korean folk tales, one will often encounter the theme of a seemingly ordinary being outwitting even the highest of authority figures. 'The Rabbit's Liver' is a prime example. Long ago, the Dragon King, who lives under the Southern Sea, was very sick. His doctors told him that the only thing that would cure his illness was the liver of a rabbit. So the Dragon King called all of his advisers together and asked who would go looking for the liver of a rabbit.

The humble turtle volunteered. He swam to the world of the land, where he came up to a sandy beach and found a rabbit. 'I have been sent by the Dragon King,' the turtle said. 'He has invited you to come and be his guest in the Dragon Palace.' The rabbit accepted the invitation. He sat on the turtle's back and they swam down to the bottom of the Southern Sea. He was excited to see all of the magnificent sights, but when they reached the palace and stood before the Dragon King, it didn't take long for the rabbit to learn that he had been tricked.

'I regret that I must eat your liver to regain my health,' said the Dragon King. 'I give you my thanks now before my doctors take you

Spectators smoking long-stemmed pipes. Two of them are standing on *jige* carriers and one wears a stylish modern cap.

away.' At first the rabbit was scared, but he was clever. 'Your Majesty,' he said, 'I would be honoured to be the one who cures you. But I'm afraid my liver is a very valuable organ, and so I keep it safely hidden in a secret place in the forest. If you will have the turtle take me back to the surface, I will gladly return with my liver.' The Dragon King was very impressed by the rabbit's devotion and honesty, and so he ordered the turtle to take him back. When they arrived once again at the beach where the turtle had found him, the rabbit hopped off the turtle's back. 'Thank you for the ride,' he said. 'Did you think I was really going to let your stupid Dragon King cut me open and take my liver?' And the clever rabbit dashed off into the forest.

Outwitting the powerful and wealthy is not only a major theme in the realm of animal stories when it comes to Korean folk tales; it is also a common theme in stories about people, which often feature explorations of class dynamics. 'The Clever Slave' is one such story. Its protagonist is the slave of a wealthy magistrate who repeatedly tricks his master out of greater and greater things, from a bowl of

A wooden rabbit and turtle doll, made some time after the Japanese colonial era.

bean soup at the story's opening (by pretending he had a runny nose and had gotten snot in it) to marrying the magistrate's daughter (by forging an official note that says the slave is to marry her). Finally, he tricks his master and his wife into killing themselves by drowning, convincing them they will end up in the Dragon King's underwater palace. While this is fundamentally a story about a member of the lower class taking revenge on his master, no class of people is spared – the clever slave also tricks various merchants and a monk along the way.

However, cleverness is not reserved for outwitting authority in Korean folklore. Intelligence was (and is) highly valued in Korean society, epitomized in the culture of the civil service exam, which led to many stories valuing the quick thinking of Confucian students. One of these, 'The Clever Student', is a folk tale about a teacher's most clever student manipulating a widow into becoming the teacher's wife by convincing the entire village the two are already having an affair. This story also addresses the visit to China that Korean Confucian scholars were expected to make during their careers. Another folk tale, 'The Mast of Sand', tells how the Korean king's prime minister, Hwang Hui, outwitted the Chinese emperor. When the emperor sends a letter to the king asking him to send a ship with all the waters of the Han River to China, Hwang Hui tells the king to reply that he would be happy to, but that the ship used to transport the water would need to have a mast of sand. Therefore, the emperor would first have to send to Korea a 300-foot mast of sand made from the deserts north of China.

One of the best illustrations of the central Confucian virtue of literacy is the story of the master calligrapher Han Ho (한호 / 韓濩; 1543–1605), better known by his penname, Seok-bong (석봉 / 石峯,

Admiral Yi and His Turtle Ships

Yi Sun-sin (이순신 / 李舜臣 1545–1598) was a Korean naval commander during the Joseon dynasty, who had studied Confucian philosophy and military science before passing the military examination in 1576. He is best known for his stunning victories against the Japanese navy during the Imjin War of 1592 to 1598. The Koreans were poorly equipped compared to the Japanese, and the Japanese invasion force was looking forward to a quick victory, especially at sea. But Yi was a brilliant naval strategist, using the manoeuvrability of the smaller Korean ships and his knowledge of the local islands and waterways to defeat the Japanese in battle after battle. He is said to have been so strong that it took two men to carry each of the two swords he used in battle, but Yi is known primarily for his cleverness.

A statue of Admiral Yi in Gwanghwamun Plaza, Seoul, near the statue of King Sejong in the same plaza (see p. 17).

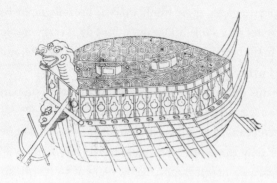

A woodblock print depicting a 16th-century turtle boat, 1795.

Yi invented a new type of war vessel, the highly manoeuvrable turtle ship, which was heavily armoured. The hull of the turtle ship was covered with iron spikes, and the deck was covered with a roof that was made of iron plates, protecting the sailors from arrows and gunfire, and had a small hole in the centre for a cannon. The turtle ship also had a number of cannons mounted on the sides and the front. Its fearsome design, which made it look like a fire-breathing dragon-turtle, struck fear into the hearts of the superstitious and demoralized Japanese sailors, particularly when it was used to ram the Japanese ships' wooden hulls and spew fire into them through its jaws. Yi's naval victories have become legendary: at the Battle of Myeongnyang in 1597, Yi's small fleet of thirteen ships defeated a Japanese fleet more than ten times its size. At the Battle of Noryang in 1598, allied with Ming Chinese admiral Chen Lin, Yi's combined fleet of 150 ships defeated a Japanese fleet of 500.

Yi Sun-sin is one of Korea's greatest national heroes and also considered to be one of the greatest naval commanders in history. His 17-metre-tall (55¾-ft) statue, with a small turtle ship beneath it, looks out over Seoul's Gwanghwamun Plaza.

meaning 'Stone Peak'). Han Seok-bong's family was so poor they couldn't afford rice paper, so he would practise his calligraphy by writing with water on a stone bridge or on the lids of earthenware jars at home. In the heat of the sun, the words would evaporate, and then he would write them again.

Eventually, his widowed mother, who sold rice cakes to support him, made him leave home and go to the mountains to study calligraphy for ten years. But he missed his mother so much that he returned after only three years, bragging that he had learned all there was to learn about calligraphy. On the night of his return, his mother tested him by putting out the lamp. 'I bet I can slice rice cakes without the light,' she told him. 'Let's see how well you've learned

An example of the Eight Principles of *Yong* (永), a method of practising the different types of calligraphic strokes, all of which are present in that single character.

your calligraphy.' In the dark, Seok-bong could hear the regular thumps on the cutting board as his mother sliced the long white rice cakes into little oval discs. When he turned the lamp back on, he saw that his mother's rice cakes were neatly sliced, but his calligraphy was an uneven mess. His mother scolded him and sent him back to the mountain to finish his remaining seven years of study, and he went on to become one of the greatest calligraphers of the Joseon era.

FEMALE VIRTUE

As alluded to throughout this book, female virtue is a pervasive theme of Korean folk tales. In the stories of virtuous women explored in this section, women endure both immense suffering and exploitation while also displaying great strength, intellect and compassion. They navigate a world in which they are expected to give everything for their families and to serve the men in their lives (from fathers, to husbands, to sons), and still remain powerful throughout. A great example is the famous story of Shimcheong.

Once, there lived a blind scholar named Shim Hakkyu. He and his wife, Gwakssi, were childless for a long time. Only after much devoted prayer did Gwakssi give birth to a beautiful girl, Shimcheong, but alas, it was too hard on Gwakssi's body due to her old age and she passed away. Shim Hakkyu did his best to raise their daughter alone, but together they endured great hardship. Shimcheong was a very obedient and virtuous daughter, and from the moment she could speak, she went out to beg for alms with her father.

One day, while Old Man Shim was out begging, he fell into an irrigation ditch. As he struggled in the water, trying and failing to climb out as he cursed his disability, he heard a voice above him. 'Old man,' it said, 'I have heard you lamenting your blindness. If you will give three hundred sacks of rice to my temple as a tribute to the Lord Buddha, we will offer up our prayers to return your sight.' Hands from Heaven itself seemed to reach down and pull Shim up and out of the water. He was so thankful that he cried, 'Thank you, kind monk! I will give you those three hundred sacks of rice! I swear it!' It was only later, when his elation wore off, that he realized he had no means of giving the temple even three bowls of rice – let alone three hundred sacks. That night, he told his daughter he had been so swept up in being treated kindly for once that he had gotten carried away, and now he was worried about what terrible fate would befall them if he offended the Buddha. As Shimcheong lay on her thin bed mat, she tried but failed to think of a way to get the rice. But in her dreams, her mother told her, 'Go to the harbour. There, you will find a merchant looking for a young maiden. Go with him and he will provide the three hundred sacks of rice.'

It turned out that the Dragon King of the East Sea was displeased with the merchant fleet, and had sent storms to sink their ships. To appease the Dragon King, the captain had agreed to sacrifice a young maiden, but no family was willing to sell their daughter. So when Shimcheong came forward and offered herself in exchange for the tribute for her father, he was happy to accept. The three hundred sacks of rice were given to the temple, but Old Man Shim didn't immediately regain his sight. The monks said it wouldn't happen overnight. Now, he'd lost his sight, his wife and his only daughter.

The weather grew stormy; the sea seemed to boil, lightning flashed and the boats' oars and chains snapped in the violent waves. The captain sent Shimcheong out onto the deck dressed in wedding finery. Although Shimcheong said she would leap into the waves of her own free will, the sailors didn't believe her, and had her hands and feet bound. When she said a quiet prayer and leaped overboard, everyone cried at the sight of her filial piety and bravery.

Shimcheong descended, and the ocean was suddenly filled with bright light. She discovered that she could breathe. She gazed in wonder as the Dragon King's servants released her and escorted her to the underwater palace. She dwelt happily there, and it was said that her mother's spirit also resided there. But eventually, she longed to see her father again, and she became deeply sad. When the Dragon King noticed, he told her, 'I cannot bear to see your unhappiness any longer, Shimcheong. I have seen that your filial piety and your selfless devotion are far greater than that of any other mortal I have known. It touches my heart to see your concern for your poor father, so as a reward for your devotion, I will send you back up into the world above.' With this, he transformed her into a giant lotus flower.

This giant white lotus blossom was found floating at the mouth of a river along the coast, and a local fisherman was so amazed by its beauty that he made it a gift to the king. The king had been recently widowed and was mournful, and it was hoped that the gift would lift his spirits. The king's eyes lit up when he first beheld the giant flower. He rewarded the fisherman handsomely and had the lotus installed in its own special room, where he would stand for hours each day in a melancholy mood, admiring its beauty. And every night, Shimcheong would emerge from the flower, then go back inside when dawn broke. One moonlit night, the king was restless, and wandered to the blossom's chamber. He stepped inside to gaze at the flower, but what he saw was even more wonderful – a woman whose beauty took his breath away. 'Who are you?' he asked. 'Are you a ghost, or are you real?'

'It is only I,' said Shimcheong. 'I who live in the giant flower.' She tried to hide herself out of modesty, but when she turned she found the lotus had vanished. She became the king's bride, and there was a lavish wedding. They spent their days together with great happiness. But one day the king saw Shimcheong weeping in the garden. 'My dear wife,' he said, 'I cannot bear to see your tears. Tell me your wish – any wish – and it shall be granted.'

'There is only one thing I desire,' she replied. 'Let there be a great public banquet in honour of our marriage, and let all the blind men of the kingdom participate in the feast. This will make my heart glad.'

The King honoured her strange request, and for three days blind men from all corners of the kingdom came to drink and dine. The queen watched through a silk curtain, but she still did not see her father.

On the last day, as the gates were closing and she was turning sadly away, there was a great racket. The servants were turning away a blind beggar who had arrived too late. Just then, the queen happened to glance backwards, to see that under the dirt and tattered rags, the old man was her father. 'Father!' she cried. 'Father! It is my dear father! Let him in!' Old Man Shim staggered inside, nearly losing his balance from the shock of hearing his daughter's voice. 'Shimcheong! Is it a ghost, or have the dead come back to life? My daughter! Is that your voice I hear? Let's have a look at you, girl!' Just as he had once before, in his enthusiasm he forgot his circumstances. Oblivious to his own blindness, he opened his eyes wide and found he could see. Before him was his daughter, more beautiful than he could have imagined. Shim Hakkyu wept with joy and embraced her, and she, too, was tearful with joy. Soon there was a happy commotion throughout the palace, and it is said that every blind man there who wanted to have a look at Shimcheong, the filial daughter, had his vision restored that day.

Shimcheong's story has much in common with the story of Princess Bari (see pp. 65–67), featuring the many trials undertaken by a virtuous daughter in the name of healing her father, including going overboard into the ocean and marrying powerful male figures on their quests. The two tales likely draw from the same source. Shimcheong's story is also particularly powerful for its Korean audience because it has elements that appeal to every prominent Korean religious tradition. Shimcheong parallels Bari, the mythical origin of the Korean shaman, and she is willing to give up everything for her father, appealing to Confucian ideals. The Dragon King, a Taoist figure, is portrayed sympathetically. While the story can at first be read to be critical of Buddhism, in the end the promise of the monk comes true, and the story could be said to represent karma. Shimcheong demonstrates the bravery, power and virtue of women while also venerating the patriarch and monarch, so that the story can appeal to people from all walks of life.

A famous Korean ghost story in the genre of wronged women that highlights Confucian values is the tale of Arang. Like Shimcheong and Princess Bari, Arang lost her mother at a young age. Unfortunately, she was raised not by her father, the magistrate of Miryang, but by a nanny who hated her. One day, her nanny conspired with a male servant who had been Arang's secret admirer and set up a secret night meeting during which he believed Arang would respond to his advances. When Arang resisted, he raped her, stabbed her to death, and buried her body in the woods. Her father was very upset at her disappearance, but thought she had simply run off with a stranger.

Every time a new magistrate was chosen, Arang's ghost would come to him and plead for help and justice, but each one was terrified and would flee from her (in some versions of the story, each magistrate is scared to death). Finally, a magistrate named Yi Sang-sa was appointed, and he wasn't afraid of ghosts. When Arang begged him for help, he promised to avenge her. He had everyone assemble in the courtyard, and Arang transformed herself into a yellow butterfly and alighted on the man who had murdered her. When Yi Sang-sa had him executed, Arang's spirit vanished, finally at peace.

Like most old legends that have been retold over generations, the story of Arang is richly layered with meaning. The new magistrate's given name, Sang-sa, would be written 상사 in *hangul*, but when it is written in *hanja*, there are several homophones that illustrate the convergence of themes in the story. Sang-sa's name is usually written 上舍, which can mean 'a living person' or someone who has passed the civil exam. He is, of course, both. He has passed the civil exam and is the only *living* magistrate after the appearance of Arang's ghost. His name also sounds like 上司, which means 'a superior' or 'a government official of a higher rank' – something he will become when he is promoted after solving the mystery. But *sangsa* can also be written 上寺, meaning a woman staying at a Buddhist temple, or a bodhisattva (a figure who responds to the suffering of others). It can be written 上祀, signifying the nation's largest ancestral rite, and finally 喪死, meaning 'a mournful death'. Yi Sang-sa behaves like a bodhisattva, relieving Arang's suffering and he performs a figurative ancestral rite. The story itself is about a mournful death. The tale of Arang thus privileges Confucianism not only by

The Green Frog

Many Korean folk tales involve the sacrifices of, and filial piety owed towards, mothers. One of the most famous folk tales on this theme is the story of a small green frog who always does the exact opposite of what his mother tells him. When she grows old and knows she will die soon, she realizes that if she wants her son to bury her properly on the mountain, she will have to use reverse psychology. She makes him promise to bury her on the bank of a river instead. But when she dies, her son regrets never having listened to her while she was alive, and finally does what she told him to do. So it is said that now, whenever there is a heavy rain, the green frog is afraid that his mother's grave will be swept away, and that is why frogs cry when it rains.

A painting of a frog from an album of art
by Joseon-era artist Baek Eun-bae.

casting a model Confucian as the hero, but also by revealing its own linguistic and symbolic sophistication to those who are literate in Confucian culture.

Another way to communicate the qualities that a culture considers 'ideal' is to contrast a virtuous woman with a cruel woman. One folk tale that does this is the story of Kongjwi and Patjwi, sometimes called the 'Korean Cinderella' in the West. Kongjwi is a poor girl who is treated like a slave by her stepmother and her stepsister, Patjwi. With help from spirits – including the spirit of her dead mother in the form of a cow, in older versions of the tale – she ends up winning the heart of a magistrate, and lives in luxury as his wife for a time. But her stepsister grows jealous, and one day pretends to have changed her ways. When Kongjwi forgives her, Patjwi convinces her to swim with her in a lotus pond, and then drowns her there. Patjwi disguises herself as Kongjwi and lives her life for a while, but before long Kongjwi's spirit returns, taking the form of a lotus that psychologically torments her sister by seeming to stare at her and by becoming the magistrate's new obsession. Simultaneously, Kongjwi also takes the form of beads that are taken home by an old woman who was Kongjwi's friend in life. Eventually, the old woman and Kongjwi's spirit work together to expose Patjwi. The magistrate is furious when he learns that he has been tricked, and orders that Patjwi be beaten, torn apart and finally her remains pickled in a jar and sent back to her mother.

One of Korea's most famous love stories, *The Tale of Chunhyang* (춘향전 / 春香傳), features a bond between mother and daughter and the theme of hypergamy (upward mobility via marriage). Its original authorship is unknown, but it was adapted into prose during the seventeenth or eighteenth century. The eponymous Chunhyang

(춘향 / 春香, normally glossed as 'Spring Fragrance', but also containing the more suggestive meanings 'lust/youthful/joyous fragrance') is the daughter of a *gisaeng* (기생 / 妓生) – a courtesan. *Gisaeng* were women trained to be highly cultured entertainers – much like their Japanese counterpart, the geisha – but were at the bottom rung of the Confucian social hierarchy. In spite of this, Chunhyang's mother manages to marry a minister, meaning that her daughter Chunhyang is not a *gisaeng* herself.

Changing Endings

Much of the initial cataloguing of Korean folklore began during the Japanese colonial era (1910–45) as part of a programme to study Korean culture, with the ultimate aim of eradicating it by having Koreans assimilate into Japanese language and culture. So it is an irony that, for folklorists, many of the earliest scholarly collections of Korean folk tales were compiled by Japanese anthropologists and sociologists. Given the time and the politics of that era, it is understandable that the general tone of those collected stories would be pessimistic or fatalistic.

Later collections of folk tales from post-liberation Korea tend to have a distinctly different tone, and many of the same stories have different, more optimistic (and sometimes even traditionally 'happy') endings. After the 'economic miracle' of the 1970s through the 1990s, there is an even greater move towards optimism.

One example of this transformation can be seen in the story of 'Kongjwi and Patjwi'. In the colonial era, the story included the second half, in which Kongjwi's jealous stepsister murders her and takes her place with Kongjwi's husband, but in recent years the story typically ends happily with Kongjwi's marriage to the wealthy magistrate, in much the same way *Grimms' Fairy Tales* have been edited in modern retellings to remove dark and disturbing material.

Yi Mong-ryong, the son of the local magistrate, immediately falls in love with Chunhyang when he sees her on a swing. Chunhyang doesn't respond to his attempts to court her at first, but when he asks her mother for permission to marry her daughter it is granted, because Chunhyang could secure a better life for herself by marrying up and being a respectable wife. Yi Mong-ryong is not able to marry, however, until he has completed his civil service exams. While watching him study, Chunhyang falls in love with him. They are happy together for a time, but when Yi Mong-ryong's father is promoted to a position in the capital in Hanyang (what is now Seoul), Chunhyang is not permitted to follow him, due to her lower status. Yi Mong-ryong promises her that he will pass his exams and be promoted to a high position himself, and then he will return to her. Chunhyang gives him a ring as a sign of her love and faithfulness.

The magistrate who replaces Mong-ryong's father is cruel, lazy and licentious. He demands that Chunhyang be his personal *gisaeng* and sleep with him, and when she refuses because she is a married woman, he has her tortured and thrown in prison. Just as she is on the brink of death, her love returns. He has received the highest score on the civil examination and is now a secret royal inspector working undercover to expose political corruption (a highly coveted position). He hears stories throughout the region of the virtuous Chunhyang and the man who abandoned her. Disguised in rags as a beggar, he exposes the corrupt magistrate and frees Chunhyang and others who were wrongfully imprisoned. While still disguised and unrecognized by Chunhyang, he tests her to see if she is still faithful to him by asking her to be his *gisaeng*. When she refuses him, he shows her the ring she gave to him. *The Tale of Chunhyang* illustrates the virtues that women in Korea were expected to aspire to, the hypocrisy of those who abuse their power, and also the wishful desire of common people to move upward in social status.

The previous folk tales in this section feature virtues valued by Korea's Neo-Confucian culture. However, there are folk tales that are critical of these values and of patriarchy – one such story is even told in the *Samguk Sagi* (see p. 42). 'Ondal the Fool', a pseudohistorical origin story of one of the princes of Goguryeo, is about Princess Pyeonggang (평강공주 / 平岡公主). Since she was young, whenever she misbehaved, her father, the king of Goguryeo, would make her cry by telling her she would end up marrying the village fool, a boy named Ondal (온달 / 溫達). When she comes of age and her father tries to arrange a suitable marriage for her, she refuses and is exiled for it. She decides, out of spite, to go to Ondal's house and convince Ondal and his blind mother that she should marry him. The princess uses her money to help Ondal's family, and then she teaches her husband how to ride on horseback and eventually how to become a great general and strategist.

POVERTY AND SACRIFICE

Sacrifice isn't the sole domain of virtuous women in Korean folk tales. While there are plenty of stories and even biographies that feature impoverished mothers so devoted that they make pudding out of their own blood to feed their sons who are studying for the civil examination, enduring suffering and being rewarded for it – even without the use of trickery – is a recurring theme illustrated by characters of all genders. The self-sacrificing men are often younger siblings, as in 'The Goblin's Club'. In Korean folk tales, it is very common for people to be referred to by their role or archetype instead of by name. Even in daily life, people tend to be known by their occupation, relation to another person, or a physical feature. In the following story, the main characters are referred to by their roles as younger and older brothers only.

Once there lived two brothers. The rich, older brother was spoiled and selfish, while the poor, younger brother was a filial, hardworking woodcutter. Each day, he rose at the crack of dawn to go into the hills and gather wood. One day, he'd worked especially hard, and as he was resting under a tree, an acorn fell beside him. 'This one's for my father,' he said, and picked it up. Another acorn fell, and another, and another. He picked them up and said, 'This one's for my mother. This one's for my older brother. This one's for his wife.' He put the acorns in his pocket and got his load of wood to carry back home.

Bad Names

The practice is less common in contemporary urban Korea, but traditionally, just about every neighbourhood would have children whose names were 'Piggy' or 'Dog Shit'. Their mothers would be known as 'Piggy's Mother' or 'Dog Shit's Mother'. 'Piggy' was a nickname given for its auspicious qualities, since Koreans believe that pigs are a sign of affluence (and seeing a pig in a dream – having a 'pig dream' – is good fortune). 'Dog Shit', on the other hand, signifying the lowliest of low things, is a nickname usually given to an especially attractive boy in order to keep the spirits from doing him harm out of envy or jealousy. The children generally outgrow their nicknames when they become teenagers, but because mothers are traditionally referred to in relation to their firstborn, the mothers are sometimes stuck with their names for life.

Darkness fell suddenly, and frightened by the eerie calls of the cuckoo, the younger brother lost his way. After the longest time, he found an abandoned house in the woods. He was so tired that he went inside, but he was plagued by anxious thoughts and could not sleep. He was tossing and turning when he heard gruff voices and a loud commotion. Quickly, he hid inside a closet.

Just then, a gang of goblins came into the room! Each of them held a large wooden club. They gathered in a circle and beat the floor. 'Make gold! *Ttukk! Ttakk!*' they shouted, and a pile of gold appeared on the floor. 'Make silver! *Ttukk! Ttakk!*' they chanted, and a pile of silver appeared.

The younger brother was terrified, afraid to make even the smallest noise. But even in his terror, he was hungry, and his stomach rumbled. Instantly, the goblins stopped their chanting. 'What was that sound?' one asked. They all looked around. 'Thunder,' said another. 'Let us hurry before rain comes. The roof is leaky on this old shack.'

When the goblins started again, the younger brother realized he was doomed if his stomach rumbled again. He had to eat something to quiet it. He searched his pockets and found the acorns. As quietly as possible, he put one in his mouth and gently bit down. There was a loud crack! The goblins scattered in terror. 'Get out! It's the roof beam!'

The woodcutter's heart had nearly exploded from fright. He remained in the closet all night, and it was only at sunrise that he came out and found the piles of gold, silver and jewels. He gasped, but eventually came to his senses. He unloaded the wood and loaded up his A-frame with as much treasure as he could carry instead. He noticed a goblin had dropped a magic club, too, so he took that as well.

He became the richest man in town, used the treasure to build a palatial house and invited his parents to live there with him. Whenever he needed money, he just used the club and said the magic words. But the woodcutter's older brother was terribly jealous. He visited his younger brother and asked him for the story behind his wealth. The younger brother happily told him, but the older brother wasn't really listening – only imagining the treasure and wealth he could obtain.

That night, the older brother put on his oldest clothes, put on his A-frame, chopped a load of firewood as fast as he could, then sat under the oak tree as described. An acorn fell. 'An acorn for me,' he said. Then another fell, and another, and another. 'Another one for me, another for me to eat!' he exclaimed. Pockets full of acorns,

A man adjusts his load of rice-straw sacks that he is carrying on a *jige* (A-frame) carrier.

he set off on his way. The sky grew dark, and he heard the cuckoo crying. But he wasn't terrified like his brother had been. He took off his A-frame and went into the shack, then waited impatiently. It felt like it took forever for the goblins to arrive.

As soon as the goblins began their game, he couldn't wait any longer. He bit into an acorn with a loud crack.

'So, the greedy fool has returned!' a goblin said. 'He tricked me out of my magic club last time. Let's teach him a lesson!' The goblin jerked the closet door open, and the man tumbled out. The goblins beat him mercilessly. 'Flatten him! *Ttukk! Ttakk!*' and when the club landed, he flattened like a blanket. 'Stretch him! *Ttukk! Ttakk!*' and the brother became long and thin like a bamboo pole. All night, the goblins had their fun with him. At dawn, they finally left, leaving him long and thin. The older brother put his A-frame over his thin, gangly shoulders and staggered back home.

For a culture in which people often had less than they needed to subsist, stories of sacrifice and unexpected wealth serve the important functions of reinforcing social control or acting as escapism. This story serves both purposes. Given the Korean idealization of Confucianism, it may be surprising to see that one of the story's central characters is a wicked older brother, but then folk tales are usually told by and for the common people. Just as many Korean folk tales are critical of authority, so too are they critical of many aspects of the Neo-Confucian social order and how it can result in exploitation and abuses of power. Despite this critical nature, 'The Goblin's Club' also helps propagate the system – it suggests that even if someone you are supposed to venerate is wicked and greedy, as long as you retain your Confucian virtues, outside forces will eventually punish the wrongdoer.

NORTH KOREA: THE REAL HERMIT KINGDOM

In 1948, three years after the Korean peninsula was liberated from Japanese colonial rule and divided along the 38th parallel by the Soviet Union and the United States, North Korea officially became the Democratic People's Republic of Korea (the DPRK). Yet the DPRK is not democratic, nor is it a 'people's republic', and the people call themselves 'Joseon' people, referring to the period and the nation under the rule of the Yi-dynasty kings. North Korea is largely built on the myth of its own Kim dynasty, beginning with its updating of ancient foundation myths via the use of propaganda and consolidated by the development of the ideology of *Juche* (주체), which emphasizes self-reliance and independence. In many ways, North Korea remains the mythic 'Hermit Kingdom', and because information coming from it is inherently unreliable, it is especially useful to view it through a mythic lens.

In 2011, Kim Jong-il died, and his son Kim Jong-un assumed power. Kim Jong-un continued his predecessors' policies, emphasizing military strength and nuclear development. His leadership has been marked by a combination of increased international tension, human rights abuses, and a push for economic development through limited market reforms.

In the late twentieth century, North Korea's relations with the outside world were strained. The country's pursuit of nuclear

Juche Sasang (주체사상 / 主體思想)

Juche Sasang – 'Self-reliance Ideology' or 'Self-reliance Thought' –
is North Korea's official state ideology, though it is often referred
to as its political philosophy. It was introduced by Kim Il-sung as a
guiding principle for the country's governance. Under *Juche* ideology
the nation was to be self-reliant in all aspects of its development,
including its economy, culture and military, and maintain
independence from outside influences, particularly from major
powers like the United States and the Soviet Union (later Russia).
Juche calls for a strong sense of national identity, loyalty to the ruling
party and leader, and an unwavering commitment to the sovereignty
of the state. The practical implementation of *Juche* has included
policies aimed at reducing dependency on foreign aid, developing
domestic industry, and emphasizing indigenous technologies,
but has resulted in economic isolation, the harsh limiting of
individual freedoms and severe punishment of any dissent.

The Chinese characters that form the word can be read as
'God's Body' or 'Divine Body', suggesting that Kim chose that
particular term for its resonance with the idea of the people and the
nation forming one divine body with its own integrity. This is much
like the Christian idea of the people constituting the Church, which
is then characterized as the body of Christ, who is God. In North
Korea, the divine figure would be Kim Il-sung. Kim's grandfather was
a Protestant minister and his father was a Presbyterian elder, so it is
no surprise that he would incorporate Christian symbolism into his
political ideology. The Chinese character 主 in *Juche* sounds just like
the *Ju* in Kim Il-sung's birth name, Kim Song-ju. That *Ju* (柱) is made
of the *ju* for 'God' with the addition of the wood radical 木 on the left,
making it mean 'pillar'. Its mnemonic is 'wooden lord' (as in the
power that holds up a house). Kim Il-sung must have purposely
used that homophone to add yet another layer of connection between
himself and the body of the state, and it may be no accident that the
wood radical 木 has a cross in it.

weapons and long-range ballistic missiles led to tensions with the international community, particularly the United States and its allies. Despite diplomatic efforts to curb North Korea's nuclear ambitions, the country conducted its first successful nuclear test in 2006.

North Korea's stringent and self-imposed isolation has made it difficult to gather accurate information about the country's internal affairs. It remains an enigmatic nation, and there are currently signs of an amplification of its withdrawal from the world even while the use of global media is becoming more sophisticated under the rule of Kim Jong-un.

KIM IL-SUNG 김일성 金日成

Kim Il-sung (1912–1994), the founding leader of North Korea, adopted a centralized command economy, with strong ties to the Soviet Union and communist China and heavily dependent on their aid. Ironically, under his rule, the country pursued the ideology of *Juche*. Kim was portrayed in a highly idealized and mythologized way, known during his lifetime as the 'Great Leader' and now as 'The Eternal Leader' and 'Eternal President'. The North Korean regime created a cult of personality around him, which involved the creation of legends and myths to enhance his image as a heroic and all-powerful leader.

The best-known of these is regarding the narrative of his birth. Kim, whose birth name was Kim Song-ju (김성주 / 金成柱), was actually born in 1912 near Pyongyang in the village of Chilgol near the Taedong River (where the American merchant ship the *General Sherman* had run aground in 1866 in its disastrous attempt to open up trade with Korea). But according to the official North Korean narrative, he was born in a log cabin on Mount Paektu (Baeku) – the highest peak on the Korean Peninsula – the birthplace of Dangun, the mythic founder of the Korea of antiquity (see p. 46). Kim's birth is said to have been heralded by the miraculous appearance of a bright star, a sky full of lightning and double rainbows.

During Japanese colonial rule, Kim is said to have been a leader of the Korean People's Liberation Army, known for his bravery and his brilliant tactics in fighting and defeating the Japanese, including an episode in which he used *chukjibeop*, his ability to fold space, to teleport and outmanoeuvre them. He was known as the 'Tiger of Mount Paektu' and later the 'Heaven-sent Saint Bringing all Blessings to the People'. It is said that he could chop down a tree with a single swipe of his mighty sword (an allusion to Siddhartha, the young Buddha), that he crossed a river by walking on leaves (an allusion to the Buddhist monk Bodhidharma, who brought Buddhism to the East), and that he destroyed an American tank single-handedly by transforming a pine cone into a hand grenade.

Kim is said to have written hundreds of novels, which is unlikely, to say the least, but he was in fact very much interested in the power of novels to function as propaganda and sway the hearts of the people. He was a good friend of Han Sorya (한설야, 1900–1976), who is considered today – even in South Korea – to be one of the most important writers in modern Korean history for his role as Kim's propagandist, contributing enormously to the construction of his cult of personality. It was Han who first described Kim as 'Our Sun' and as 'The Sun of the Nation'. Han was later purged and there were attempts to erase his legacy, but he may have been instrumental in the writing of Kim's famous *Juche* speech and was certainly influential in Kim's understanding of the power of language.

Kim took the name 'Kim Il-sung' in 1935. It has been interpreted to mean 'Kim Become the Sun', but the wordplay and symbolism are far more complex and relevant to his mythification. As part of their policy to remain linguistically 'pure', North Koreans generally do not use Chinese characters (their use was officially abolished in 1949), but because his name was constructed before the nation existed, they are known to be KIM 金 IL 日 and SEONG 成. 金 can be read as 'gold' or 'metal'; 日 can be read as 'sun', 'day' or 'one' (or 'unifying' or 'single'); and 成 is read as 'to succeed', 'to accomplish' or 'to become'. His name thus has a wide spectrum of symbolic resonance, from becoming the golden sun (i.e., the day star), to being the one who accomplishes unification through the use of metal (i.e., industrial development). The last Chinese character, *seong*, also sounds like 星, which literally means 'star', suggesting that the star on the North Korean flag is a representation of its leader.

There is purportedly a forbidden book in North Korea that describes a prophetic warning that Kim's father, who is said to have studied the ancient traditions, had given him. He told Kim to be wary of snakes, and that if one ever blocked his path, he should not go in that direction. Before his death in 1994, Kim had gone to Mount Myohyang and a snake had blocked the road. His bodyguards were about to kill the snake when Kim intervened and simply told the snake to go away. The snake left, and with his entourage, Kim continued on that road, disregarding his father's warning.

Following Kim Il-sung's death, North Korean state media reported that unusual natural phenomena were occurring around the world, including glowing halos around the sun and other

A Symbolic Signature?

There is a twist to the symbolism of Kim Il-sung's name, which can be seen in his signature. It is not clear whether this was wilful or simply from the vagaries of signing quickly, but the *Kim* in his handwritten signature looks more like the fraction ½ than it does the *hangul* for Kim. This ironically suggests a divided Korea even while Kim's stated goal was to unify the peninsula. Perhaps the optimistic and literary way to read the signature would be 'The unity of the two halves will one day be accomplished'. If the last character is read as the Chinese homophone 性, it could also mean 'Half of one essence'.

Note that the sign for 'Kim' (김) bears a resemblance to the ½ fraction, while the 'Il' (일) and 'Sung' (성) are quite legible.

celestial occurrences, caused by the Earth itself grieving for him. The huge crowds of people wailing to the point of collapse were an international spectacle, and many journalists doubted the authenticity of the crowds' emotions. It is important to remember that the mourning was compulsory and the depth of the mourner's grief was judged an expression of loyalty to Kim and the state. Mourners who did not show adequate emotion were reported by their comrades and could suffer penalties as extreme as a prison camp sentence. The histrionics were, therefore, ironically authentic, though the underlying emotion may have been fear more than sorrow.

Kim Il-sung's body lies in state in the Kumsusan Palace of the Sun in Pyongyang, preserved and displayed for public viewing as a continuation of his leadership and presence, suggesting that he still guides and protects the nation even after his death. He is the 'Eternal Leader', an infallible and perfect ruler who possessed a deep and compassionate connection with the people and an innate understanding of their needs, his political decisions always correct and guided by extraordinary wisdom and foresight. In reality, North Korea faced increasingly dire economic challenges during his rule owing to his policy of strict isolationism, culminating in widespread famine due to economic mismanagement, natural disasters and the collapse of the Soviet Union, which had been a major supporter, in 1991, three years before Kim Il-sung's death. Nevertheless, North Korean narratives emphasize that Kim Il-sung's legacy was carried forward by his son and successor, Kim Jong-il, and now by his grandson, Kim Jong-un, although they will never achieve his status as the 'Eternal Leader' who watches over the nation even from the afterlife.

KIM JONG-IL 김정일 金正日

Like his father, Kim Jong-il, the second leader of North Korea, was also subject to a cult of personality that included the creation of legends and myths of supernatural occurrences in order to maintain his image as a revered and almost god-like figure.

Records show that Kim Jong-il was born in Siberia, but the official North Korean accounts state that he was born in a log cabin on Mount Paektu after a swarm of swallows flew around the guerrilla camp, foretelling his arrival. A bright star was also seen in the heavens, echoing the birth narrative of Kim Il-sung. It is said that Kim Jong-il was precocious and prodigious (as a good Confucian should be) – that he was already walking at three weeks and able to talk at eight weeks, and that he wrote 1,500 books while he was at university and penned six full operas. It is said that he would inspect every grain of rice served to him for perfection, that he invented the hamburger (calling it 'layered bread with meat'), that his military-style suits started a global fashion trend, and that he never needed to use the toilet because he had developed his metabolism in superhuman ways. One of the stranger claims made about Kim Jong-il is that when he turned North Korea's clocks back by half an hour on his father's birthday in 2015, he was literally reclaiming the time that the Japanese had stolen from Korea during their occupation.

Like Kim Il-sung, Kim Jong-il was depicted as having unparalleled wisdom and intellect. His decisions were portrayed as infallible, and his guidance was believed to be crucial for the nation's success. But perhaps because he was the successor to a divine figure, Kim Jong-il never achieved the same level of adulation as his father. He would be known as the 'Dear Leader' and 'Great Comrade', and 'Great Successor'. Just before Kim Jong-il's death, it is said that the skies turned red above Mount Paektu, and that huge cracks appeared in the sheet of ice that covered Heaven Lake in the volcanic crater at the top of the mountain.

North Korean propaganda often highlighted Kim Jong-il's supposed mastery in various fields, from military strategy to literature and film-making. He was portrayed as a polymath who excelled in every endeavour he pursued, yet he was the leader during the 'Arduous March' of the mid- to late 1990s, a period of great crisis plagued by natural disasters and famine that followed the collapse of North Korea's ally and supporter, the Soviet Union. North Korea's isolationism only amplified the problems, highlighting a major weakness in the ideology of *Juche*. It is reported that more than three million people died of starvation and related illnesses during the famine, much of the news being reported by those who escaped into China and then sought refuge in South Korea.

While his father believed the novel to be the most elevated form of propaganda, Kim Jong-il turned his attention to poetry, children's books, comics and especially film. Part of this was due to simple economic pressure: there was a paper shortage, which made it prohibitive to disseminate large numbers of novels. Among the thousands of essays and books attributed to Kim Jong-il are instructive tracts on the proper *Juche*-focused aesthetics of writing and film production. His interest in children's books and comics may have been because their form overlapped with film, a visual medium with which he was authentically obsessed. He is listed as the author of *On the Art of the Cinema,* a book full of essays on topics ranging from literary and film theory to insights on directing and the creative process. In the preface he writes:

'The cinema occupies an important place in the overall development of art and literature. As such it is a powerful ideological weapon for the [socialist] revolution and construction. Therefore, concentrating efforts on the cinema, making breakthroughs and following up success in all areas of art and literature is the basic principle that we must adhere to in revolutionizing art and literature.'

Kim Jong-il was a film aficionado, and had aspirations of becoming a director. The Pyongyang Film Studio, which is more than twice the size of Paramount's studio, produced nearly 12,000 movies while he was its overseer. During his lifetime, he would also assemble a private collection of more than 20,000 films including every Oscar winner. It is said that Kim Jong-il idolized Sean Connery and followed the entire James Bond series, even after North Koreans were caricatured as the villains of *Die Another Day*. He also enjoyed American action and horror films and Japanese films of the *kaiju* (monster) genre, the *Godzilla* films being some of his all-time favourites.

Pulgasari: **North Korea's** *Godzilla*

Films had the ability to reach a large audience more quickly and effectively than novels, since they could be circulated out to the countryside, and were screened as a monthly treat for large audiences of villagers who could not afford to buy – or have the leisure time to read – novels. Comic books and illustrated children's books served not only a domestic function, but were also exported for sale. Where illustration and film intersected, animation proved to be a significant economic asset, and North Korea became, for a time, the animation sweatshop of the world.

In 1978, Kim Jong-il kidnapped the famous South Korean actress Choi Eun-hee after luring her to Hong Kong for a business meeting. When her former husband, the director Shin Sang-ok, went to Hong Kong to look for her, he was also kidnapped as part of Kim Jong-il's plan to have them make propaganda films for North Korea.

A still from the 1967 South Korean science fiction film
Space Monster Wangmagwi, as the monster terrorizes Seoul.

Shin was imprisoned for more than two years for not cooperating and trying to escape. In 1983 he was brought to Pyongyang, where he was compelled to remarry Choi and began making movies. He would make seven films for Kim Jong-il, including an adaptation of the classic folk tale, *The Tale of Shim Chong*, but the one he is remembered for – and perhaps the most famous North Korean film in the outside world – is the 1985 *kaiju* film *Pulgasari*. *Pulgasari* was originally a 1962 South Korean film – now lost – which was a critical and commercial flop when it was released, but it had made an impression on Kim Jong-il for its mythic and allegorical resonance. Its 1985 remake by Shin Sang-ok amplifies its symbolic and allegorical qualities in a way that is uniquely tailored for North Korea while also containing what is perhaps Shin Sang-ok's private symbolic critique of the Kim dynasty.

Pulgasari is a historical piece set during the time of the Goryeo dynasty. An old blacksmith is beaten, imprisoned and starved for defying the cruel governor. When his two children manage to throw him bits of rice to keep him alive, he does not eat it. Instead, he maintains a hunger strike with other peasants in the prison. Just before the blacksmith dies, he shapes a tiny monster figurine out of bits of soiled, grey rice, and prays to the gods to make the monster a defender of the people. Later, when the blacksmith's daughter accidentally pricks her finger with a sewing needle, a drop of her blood falls onto the figurine, bringing it to life. It immediately eats the needle and grows larger. Eventually, after eating kitchen utensils, farming implements and other metal objects, the creature grows into a giant monster called Pulgasari (불가사리), which means 'undying' or 'unkillable'.

The story proceeds very much like the Jewish myth of the Golem: the monster helps the local peasants defeat the evil governor. But the king's royal army is able to put a stop to the rebellion by holding the blacksmith's daughter hostage and thus forcing Pulgasari to surrender. They bury the monster in the rocky ground, making it dormant, but the blacksmith's daughter escapes one night. She brings Pulgasari back to life by cutting her arm and dropping blood into the rocky ground to feed it, and this time the monster helps the peasant army defeat the evil king.

But Pulgasari's appetite for metal is insatiable, and the people realize they cannot keep feeding it or it will consume all of their farming tools. They fear that if it grows hungry, it might become violent and turn on them. The only solution is to destroy it, but the people are helpless. Once again, the blacksmith's daughter sacrifices herself. She crawls inside a metal bell, and when Pulgasari eats it, he

---

The Emille Bell (에밀레종)

 The Emille Bell, weighing just under nineteen tons, is the largest bronze bell in Korea and is considered a masterpiece of Unified Silla art. Also known as the Sacred Bell of King Seongdeok the Great, it was commissioned in the late eighth century by his son, King Gyeongdeok. But King Gyeongdeok died before the bell could be cast and it was during the reign of his son, King Hyegong, that it was finally completed in 771 CE.

 The bell was intended as an act of devotion to be housed at Bongdeok Temple, but repeated attempts to cast it all failed. It would make no sound when it was struck. Finally, a monk came forward and revealed that when he was collecting donations for the first casting of the bell, he had approached a village woman who was so poor that she joked that the only precious thing she could offer was the infant she carried on her back. This memory had come to the monk in a dream, with the revelation that only the sacrifice of that child would allow the bell to sound properly. The king was reluctant to make a human sacrifice, but, determined to fulfil his father's dying wish, he ordered the monk to find the child.

 The bell was cast once again, and this time the young child was taken from the distraught mother and thrown into the molten bronze. When it finally cooled and the bell was hung and struck with the giant wooden rod, it made a beautiful and ethereal sound that could be

---

turns to stone. Cracks form throughout his body and he collapses into pieces, killing both himself and the girl.

The symbolism in *Pulgasari* is both blunt and sophisticated. On the one hand, it fulfils all of the requirements of Kim Jong-il's film theory, carrying out its propagandistic function of dramatizing the struggle of peasants against an oppressive government. The monster's namesake is the mythical *pulgasari*, a creature that eats metal and cannot die. Shin Sang-ok's *Pulgasari* incorporates plenty of

heard for miles: 'Emille! Emille!' – which sounded like 'Mommy!' in the ancient Silla dialect.

There are no official records of this incident, but it endured as a legend in oral tradition until it was finally recorded by Christian missionaries in the nineteenth century, during the Japanese colonial era. The Emille Bell is intricately decorated with Buddhist motifs and text that tells of its commission and casting. It is one of South Korea's most important national treasures.

The Emille Bell, which is now held at the National Museum of Gyeongju.

cinematic clichés while also alluding to classic tales like the story of Shimcheong (the blacksmith's daughter wears a blue – *cheong* – skirt when she sacrifices her blood to bring the creature back to life) and the legend of the Emille Bell (the decoration on the bell she hides in is unmistakably an allusion to its design).

At first, Kim Jong-il loved *Pulgasari*. It is, after all, superior to the typical North Korean propaganda film, and even in comparison to South Korea's contributions to the *kaiju* genre. *Pulgasari*'s production values are better than the 1967 *Space Monster Wangmagwi* (우주괴인 왕마귀), a South Korean comedy/allegory complete with rubbery monster suit, and its themes are more socially relevant than those of *Yongary, Monster from the Deep* (대괴수 용가리), released the same year and also South Korean, though it is often mistaken for a Japanese *kaiju* film. (In *Yongary*, the Godzilla-like monster emerges from the area around Panmunjom and then goes south to terrorize Seoul in a rather obvious symbolic gesture.) *Pulgasari* even holds its own against the classic Japanese monster movies, since many of the crew had worked for Toho, the studio that produced the Godzilla films. In fact, the actor who wore the Pulgasari costume had once played Godzilla.

But *pulgasari* also happens to be the common term used to refer to a starfish in Korean, and that causes the symbolism of the

Movie poster for the 1967 South Korean *kaiju* film, *Yongary, Monster from the Deep.*

168

film to undergo an unexpected twist, which Kim Jong-il might not have realized until after Shin Sang-ok and his wife escaped during a fundraising trip to Vienna. A metal-consuming monster associated with a star – that could be taken to mean Kim Il-sung, and the monster's insatiable appetite that finally threatened the lives of the agrarian peasants could represent the appetite of industrialism and development. Pulgasari, initially a saviour, had to be killed in the end via personal sacrifice. He dies after eating a bell, which in Korean is pronounced *jong* and sounds like the word for 'slave' or 'servant'. The bell is a 'metal bell', which can be written in a mix of Korean and Chinese characters as *kim jong* (金 종), also the recognized Romanization of the first two syllables of Kim Jong-il's name. This suggests that, at the end of the story, a Kim Il-sung symbol cannibalizes a Kim Jong-il symbol, destroying them both. (Of course, Shin Sang-ok would have had to deny this analysis had he remained trapped in North Korea.)

Kim Jong-il subsequently banned *Pulgasari*, but by then the monster had escaped into the world and now it can be watched – remastered in 4K and subtitled – on YouTube because it is considered to be in the public domain.

KIM JONG-UN 김정운 金正恩

Kim Jong-un, the current leader of North Korea, continues the Kim dynasty's cult of personality, particularly because of his striking and carefully cultivated resemblance to his grandfather. Like his father, Kim Jong-il, he is mythologized as a child prodigy, with exceptional achievements in academics, sports and the arts. Korean schoolchildren are taught, in classes dedicated to the leader's life, that he learned to drive at three and won a boat race against the CEO of a foreign yacht company at age nine. It is also said that, like his father's and grandfather's, his birth was heralded by a swallow and marked by supernatural signs that foretold his destiny as a leader. Generally, however, his association with supernatural phenomena seems to be de-emphasized, in keeping with the times when internet memes have begun to replace mythology.

In his efforts to modernize North Korea, Kim Jong-un has begun deliberately to demythologize some of the more implausible supernatural claims that have become common folklore regarding the previous Kims, particularly Kim Il-sung. To many outside analysts, it was a surprise to see the official state newspaper, the *Rodong Sinmun* (로동신문, literally *Labor Newspaper*) explain that while he was fighting the Japanese as a guerrilla leader, Kim Il-sung, though a brave and brilliant strategist and tactician, could not actually fold space to circle around the enemy. The article stated, 'In fact, people can't disappear and reappear by folding space.' The state has instead turned to emphasizing Kim Jong-un's continuation and expansion of his father's 'military first' policy and his expertise in media and technology, highlighting scientific achievements such as the development of nuclear weapons, particularly intercontinental ballistic missiles (ICBMs) capable of threatening the United States. In 2017, Kim Jong-un claimed to have successfully developed a hydrogen bomb. He is praised by state media for his diplomacy, even while he maintains perhaps the harshest isolationist policies since the COVID-19 pandemic, and his compassion, despite his sanctioning the murder of his older half-brother, Kim Jong-nam, and the imprisonment, torture and execution of those whom he believes to be real or potential threats to his power.

But even with the modern updating of Kim's image, there are continued symbolic gestures that associate him with the mythic past. For
example, he is part of the 'Mount Paektu Lineage', just like his father
and grandfather, and because the position of mythic founding figure
is occupied by Kim Il-sung, Kim Jong-un has been photographed
riding a white horse, aligning him with the god-king Dongmyeong
(동명 / 東明, 'Eastern Brightness') of the Goguryeo dynasty, who
was said to ride a white *girin*. As a boy, Dongmyeong was known
as Prince Chumo (see p. 51) and called 'The Son of Heaven', and he
grew up to conquer the competing kingdoms and form a unified
Goguryeo. These allusions to 'Eastern Brightness' (the rising sun),
'The Son of Heaven', and unification then associate Kim Jong-un
with the great red unifying star, just like his grandfather.

THE DEMILITARIZED ZONE

The Demilitarized Zone (DMZ) literally cuts the Korean peninsula
in half. It is a profound legacy of the Korean War and a constant
reminder – both literal and symbolic – that the war is technically
not over, having 'ended' only with an armistice. The fact that the
conflict could be reignited at any moment thus hangs over the
peninsula like a sword of Damocles, contributing to North Korea's
siege mentality, policy of isolationism and continued weapons
development, while providing a political rationale for a continued
American military presence in South Korea (which only serves
to reinforce North Korea's dedication to militarism). The former
American President Bill Clinton once described the DMZ as 'the
scariest place on Earth', and yet it is a major tourist attraction, with

more than a million visitors each year. Tourists are required to sign a safety waiver, which reads in part that their visit 'will entail the entrance into a hostile area and the possibility of injury or death as a direct result of enemy action'.

The DMZ is a 4-kilometre-wide (2.5-mile) strip of land that stretches 240 kilometres (150 miles) from east to west across the width of the peninsula, reflecting the front lines at the moment the armistice took effect. Both North and South fought literally to the very last second to gain as much territory as possible, resulting in large numbers of unnecessary casualties for the sake of a few metres of advantage. The symbolism of the DMZ, a curving line that divides the peninsula into communist North and capitalist South in the same way that the centre of the South Korean flag is divided by a curved line into a red 'north' and a blue 'south', is unavoidable. It is a major irony that the DMZ's parameters are not significantly different from the division of the peninsula along the 38th parallel before the beginning

South Korean guards at Panmunjom standing between two conference rooms, looking north at the Panmun-gak pavilion. The line dividing South and North Korea is where the gravel changes colour.

of the Korean War, at the cost of millions of lives. Given the terrible devastation suffered in the area, it is no surprise to hear stories – from soldiers and from people who live nearby – of ghosts, strange *dokkaebi* lights, unhappy spirits or even UFOs. Parts of the DMZ are said to be cursed, partially to scare off poachers from both sides who sneak in to hunt the wildlife that thrives there.

The Joint Security Area (JSA), also known as Panmunjom (and sometimes the 'Truce Village'), is the part of the DMZ where North and South conduct their diplomatic and military negotiations. The JSA is under the direction of the United Nations Command (UNC) in the south and the Korean People's Army (KPA) in the north. Since it is still technically a combat zone, command posts, observation posts, tunnels and bunkers have been built on both sides of the DMZ. The KPA and UNC forces also regularly patrol the heavily-mined area looking for infiltrators, finding, disabling and setting booby traps, and maintaining a presence to discourage incursions from the other side. It is very easy for soldiers from either side to accidentally wander across the demarcation line, because the signs that mark it date back to the 1950s; they are posted every 100 metres, but are so weathered and rusted that they are barely legible. According to the UNC, North Korean soldiers must pass an initiation test, which is to sneak into the southern part of the DMZ to an old cemetery and take back a rubbing of a tombstone to prove they had infiltrated the South. Those who are discovered by the UNC patrols will blow themselves up with hand grenades to avoid being caught and interrogated.

UNC vehicles are required to fly both a white flag and a UN flag on their vehicles, though this policy has been broken many times, including a period in the early 1970s when an American unit substituted a Jolly Roger for the white flag to antagonize the North Koreans. Breaches like this are discussed during meetings held in the blue conference buildings that run along the demarcation line just north of the 'Bridge of No Return', with each building and each conference table divided exactly down the middle by the line. Military personnel of each side guard the North and South entrances, with UNC forces in the south and North Korean soldiers in the north. Inside the conference rooms, it is permitted to cross the line, but leaving the room from the wrong exit could potentially cause an international incident, because it could be taken as a move to defect.

The 'Tree-trimming Incident' at Panmunjom

Late in the summer of 1976, two American Army officers were murdered by North Korean soldiers in the Joint Security Area while they were supervising a crew trimming a poplar tree. The incident, variously called the 'Axe Murder Incident' and the 'Tree-trimming Incident', happened only a few yards from the 'Bridge of No Return' and nearly reignited the Korean War.

The North Koreans, knowing that the tree obstructed the line of sight between a UNC observation post and a checkpoint, claimed that the tree could not be cut down without permission because it was a special tree, having been planted by Kim Il-sung himself. Yet on the day of the incident, fifteen North Korean soldiers allowed the UNC crew to begin trimming the tree before suddenly commanding them to stop. When the UNC crew ignored them, the North Koreans called twenty more soldiers, armed with clubs and crowbars, to the scene. They attacked the UNC crew after the KPA commander ordered, 'Kill the bastards!' Two of the UNC crew – Captain Arthur Bonifas and First Lieutenant Mark Barrett – were killed, one of them with the axes that had been brought for trimming the tree. Of the seventeen survivors, all but one were injured by the North Koreans.

North Korea, in its propaganda, purports to have a welcoming policy towards defectors from the capitalist South, and a mistakenly naïve belief among some in the American military is that North Korea is eager to accept any American soldier who is willing to defect, offering a life of luxury and privilege in the North. This wishful belief may have been the impetus for the 2023 incident when an American private, Travis King – who was facing disciplinary charges in the US military after having been detained by South Korean authorities for assault – joined a tourist group and ran between the conference buildings to the North to seek asylum. King

---

After the killings, the UNC mounted an incredible show of force called 'Operation Paul Bunyan' (named for the giant lumberjack of American and Canadian legend), whose goal was to avenge the American soldiers' deaths and intimidate the North Koreans. Three days after the 'Axe Murder Incident', the poplar tree was not just trimmed, it was chopped down. This symbolic act entailed a massive combined forces operation: a convoy of two dozen trucks carrying chainsaw-wielding military engineers; two platoons of infantry support; armaments including pick axe handles, pistols, M16s, M79 grenade launchers and even Claymore mines; a fleet of helicopters including half a dozen attack helicopters; B-52 Stratofortresses flying high overhead escorted by fighter jets; smaller F-111 bombers with more fighter jets; and even the deployment of one of the largest warships in history, the 50,000-ton USS *Midway*, just off the east coast. Meanwhile, the United States was on DEFCON 2 status.

North Korea's response is not fully known, but at the JSA only about 200 troops were deployed, setting up machine gun positions. The tree was chopped down without restarting the war, but relations with North Korea remained tense for a long time thereafter. The stump of the poplar tree remained until 1987, when it was removed and replaced with a stone monument to the two slain officers.

---

was expelled by the North Koreans after two months and charged with additional offences, including desertion.

There are two villages in the DMZ, permitted by both governments. In the south is Daesong-dong, known as 'Freedom Village', where only those who already lived there during the Korean War (and their descendants) are allowed to live. One of the benefits to residents is that they have access to large amounts of farmland, but they are in constant danger of North Korean infiltrators. In the 1980s, the 'flagpole war' that began in the conference room at Panmunjom was reignited outdoors when the South Korean government built a 100-metre-tall (330-ft) flagpole flying a huge, 130-kilogram (285-lb) flag.

Just over 2 kilometres (1¼ miles) north of Freedom Village is the village of Kijong-dong, also known as Pyeonghwa-ri, or 'Peace

---

The Flag Incident at Panmunjom

Some variation of the infamous 'flag incident' is a favourite of tour guides at Panmunjom, having taken on the status of a legend. The story goes that when the North Koreans and the UN first set up the conference room at Panmunjom, each side brought a flag to put on the central table. The UN's flag was modestly sized, while the North Koreans' was larger and taller. At the next meeting, the UN brought a new flag that was taller than the North Korean flag, which then provoked the North Koreans into bringing a yet taller flag. This went on until both flags reached all the way to the ceiling of the conference room. Eventually, the two sides had to go into formal negotiations to regulate a standard size for the table-top flags. They settled on a size and a height and regulated the size of the spike, which is what you see today, but if you look closely, you will note that the North Korean flag still has more levels to its pedestal.

Village' in the North and 'Propaganda Village' in the South. It is a Potemkin village of mostly empty houses with timed lighting to make it look like buildings are occupied, and although North Korea claims it is a farming village occupied by 200 happy families, it is more likely that it was once a place to quarter soldiers who manned hidden artillery positions. Its major feature is a 160-metre-tall (525-ft) flagpole that flies a 270-kilogram (595-lb) flag, built in direct response to the flagpole at Freedom Village. At one time, this was the largest flagpole in the world. The village is also known for blaring loud propaganda broadcasts southwards, particularly in times of political tension.

One of the unexpected features of the DMZ is that it has become a wildlife sanctuary. Insulated from the famine and deforestation

A Joseon-dynasty painting of peaches and a crane. Both are symbols of longevity.

in the North and the intense development in the South, the strip of land has become a refuge for many different animals, including migratory birds and species that are endangered or even thought to have been extinct on the peninsula. Among the animals spotted in the DMZ – many by soldiers on patrol – are leopard cats, black bears, golden eagles and multiple species of cranes. Because the water is less polluted, otters and Manchurian trout also live in the rivers between North and South Korea. Even the Siberian tiger and small fanged musk deer have been reported at the DMZ, adding to the narrative of a miraculous animal preserve.

There is currently a movement among international organizations to have the DMZ declared a permanent national park as a gesture of peace between North and South, which would make it one of the largest such features in the world. In 2012, South Korea tried to rebrand the DMZ as the Peace and Life Zone (PLZ), but the new label does not seem to have been successful.

GURIMCHAEK: COMIC BOOKS

One of the most interesting – and perhaps ironic – ways to uncover North Korean ideology is through the medium of comic books. This is because, despite their propaganda value and the explicit understanding that they are used as a tool of the state, they are taken less seriously – and therefore less carefully monitored – than high art or literature. This gives an outsider a unique opportunity to understand North Korea's underlying sensibilities, by examining what themes comic books concern themselves with, and how those themes are conveyed to children, to whom messages need to be made more obvious.

Watch Your Language

Because of North Korea's *Juche* ideology, its language is arguably more 'purely' Korean than the language spoken in South Korea. North Koreans, despite their self-reported literacy rate of 100 per cent in recent decades, generally do not use Chinese characters (*hanja*), whereas South Koreans will learn about 1,800 of them by the end of their public high school education.

South Koreans also use many foreign loan words, but North Koreans have tried to keep foreign words to a minimum, maintaining what is thought to be a native vocabulary wherever possible. This ironically makes them sound like country bumpkins to South Koreans. For example, 'milk' in South Korean is *uyu* (우유 / 牛乳), whereas in North Korean it is *sojeot* (소젖), to avoid using words that are associated with Chinese. For a South Korean, the humour is that *jeot* (젖) can also mean 'tit'. This is analogous to the English adoption of 'beef' and 'pork' from Norman, rather than using terms like 'cow meat' and 'pig meat' from the native Anglo-Saxon. Likewise, in South Korea, 'bread' is *bbang* (빵), which is the Korean pronunciation of the French word *pain*, borrowed via Japanese during the colonial era. North Koreans use the term *yangddeok* (양떡), which literally means 'Western rice cake', because Koreans had no equivalent of leavened bread.

The use of Japanese for daily terms (such as the names of vegetables, household utensils and common technology) lingered in South Korea well into the 1970s, while Japanese loan words were purged at least a decade earlier in the North. In South Korea, school children are taught to detect North Korean spies by listening for such small slip ups in the use of language. To South Koreans, the North Korean dialect sounds harsh and clipped, and even between the end of the Korean War in 1953 and today, the dialects have changed significantly enough that interpreters had to be used during the 2018 Olympic Winter Games in Pyeongchang so that the North and South Korean teams could communicate with each other.

In South Korea, comic books are called *manhwa* (만화 / 漫画), using the same Chinese characters as the Japanese *manga* (漫画), meaning 'whimsical'/'impromptu' 'pictures'/'drawings'. This designation made it clear that such art was not considered to be in the same cultural category as classical art, and indeed its aesthetic is often very different. Korean comic books were much influenced by those from Japan, but they have a distinct style, and their themes and genres are also quite different from their Japanese counterparts. In the 1960s, under the military dictatorship of Park Chung-hee, *manhwa* were classified as one of South Korea's 'social evils', along with alcoholism, drug addiction, gambling and prostitution. They were heavily censored, and most *manhwa* artists struggled to make a living in an endeavour widely held in low regard. Although there were famous and successful titles like Shin Dong Wu's *Hong Gildong* (1965), which dramatized the adventures of the folk hero from the seventeenth-century novel and eventually inspired one of Korea's first animated feature films, *manhwa* were generally relegated to the neighbourhood *manhwabang*, or 'comic-book room', little hole-in-the-wall stores in which comic books were rented out, since most Koreans could not afford to buy them. The *manhwabang* were the local hangouts for juvenile delinquents and boys playing hooky from school. In the evenings, teenage girls and grown women would send a male relative to the *manhwabang* to rent romance comics overnight, foreshadowing the video-tape rentals that would come in the 1980s and 1990s.

Manhwa ran the gamut of genres from social satire to science fiction, but retained their stigma until the mid-1980s, when Lee Hyun-se's *Alien Baseball Team*, a multi-volume soap opera about a team of social misfits (including mixed-race characters) became a bestselling national phenomenon and changed both the readership and the marketing of comics. But even after this sea change in the credibility of comics, which was due in part to student activists, they never became as prominent in South Korea as they are in Japan. During the oppressive Park regime, there had been more than 15,000 *manhwabang* throughout the country in the mid-1970s. By 2016, under a vastly more liberal democratic government, there were fewer than 500. In the twenty-first century, with the advent of webtoons and the partial collapse of the paper *manhwa* market, it is not clear whether any *manhwabang* remain in operation at all, apart from being featured as nostalgic museum installations.

In North Korea, on the other hand, the comic book – called *geurimchaek* (그림책), literally 'picture book' – has taken on an entirely different kind of social relevance. They are not relegated to low art or branded a 'social evil', because they serve as a major tool for disseminating state propaganda disguised as education and entertainment. Because they are cheaper to produce than film and because they can be read quickly (and do not demand the literacy level required for novels, though North Korea claims a 100 per cent literacy rate), *geurimchaek* became very popular, particularly during the rule of Kim Jong-il and through the years of the Arduous March.

One comic in particular, the 186-page *Great General Mighty Wing* (1994), stands out because it was printed in colour, whereas most *geurimchaek* were printed in single-colour line art with inks left over from other print jobs. *Mighty Wing* is precisely the sort of thing Kim Jong-un, the current leader, would have read as a preteen, and its embedded slogans reveal the sort of brainwashing he would have experienced at that age.

The year *Mighty Wing* was first published was also the year that Kim Il-sung, the 'Great Leader', died. North Korea had been receiving

A page from the 1940s South Korean historical *manhwa*, *Kojubu Samgukji* by Kim Yong-hwan.

massive amounts of food and economic aid, much of which came to an end as the Soviet Union collapsed. The famine that hit North Korea by the mid-1990s was devastating. The pattern of flooding and drought, exacerbated by climate change, resulted in the deaths of more than a quarter of a million people according to the country's official reports (with some outside estimates saying the true figure may be up to three million). By the late 1990s, only half the population had safe drinking water, and drought made it impossible to grow the crops needed to feed the starving population domestically.

Mighty Wing, the hero of the story, is a virtuous honeybee. He comes up with the idea of building an irrigation system to save the 'Garden of 1,000 Flowers' and replenish the supplies of honey – an allusion to the massive national aqueduct project that cost nearly 100,000 North Korean lives to build. But there is an ever-present outside threat: the wasp army, which had failed in an earlier attempt to conquer the honeybees because of Mighty Wing's heroic efforts. When the wasp general goes to meet his ally, the king of spiders, we see the symbolism spelled out for us. The wasps' uniforms recall those of the Japanese during the colonial era, while the spiders are shown with long noses, stereotypically associated with Americans. The spider queen's web looks remarkably similar to the UN logo, with its grid of white lines, suggesting that the spiders represent the United Nations Command.

Mighty Wing also plays with deep mythic symbolism. Bees, through their harvesting of nectar from flowers, are associated with the sun. (In Egyptian mythology, they are said to come from the tears of the Sun god, Ra.) In North Korean symbology, the sun is none other than the 'Great Leader' Kim Il-sung. The North Korean media also carefully associated both Kim Il-sung and his son, Kim Jong-il, with maternal imagery, in order to suggest that the state was both father and mother to the people. Symbolically, they are both of the solar lineage and also 'queen bees' to the nation of diligent workers. To deliver this symbolic story in comic-book form, accompanying bright illustrations with annotations that range from Aesop-like aphorisms to paranoid political slogans, demonstrates a masterful and double-edged application of *Juche* literary theory as formulated by Kim Jong-il himself.

Every page of the story includes a slogan that runs vertically down the outside margin. These range from praise of the home ('Happiness comes to a home where the flowers of laughter bloom') and homeland ('A clump of dirt from the homeland is more precious that foreign gold') to political advice: 'The enemy of a friend or the friend of an enemy – be equally wary of both'; 'The sight of

Cover of the North Korean children's *manhwa, Great General Mighty Wing* by Cho Pyong-won.

an enemy's smile: a piercing needle – his savouring of sweetness: a poison arrow'; 'Radicals and idiots are both mentally deficient'. These become increasingly paranoid and militaristic as the book continues. On the one hand, *Mighty Wing* is a poignant message to children, directed at preserving North Korea's natural resources and modelling devotion to the state; on the other, it is political indoctrination at its most insidious.

Other North Korean comic books reveal how propaganda and drama work together to carry the state's messages more subtly. *The Secret of Frequency A*, also published in 1994, is about an elite group of North Korean girl and boy scientists who save an unnamed African nation from an evil force: a mysterious sound that has created a swarm of voracious locusts, devastating the local eco-system. If it is not stopped, the result would not just be local famine, but the eventual breakdown of the global food chain.

The evil technology behind this 'Frequency A' is associated with a villainous group of characters assembled from immediately recognizable stereotypes: a hawkish figure named 'Kelton' to suggest a British official, a big-nosed American named 'Ronald', a buck-toothed Japanese scientist in the requisite Coke-bottle glasses, and a Nazi war criminal. The technology they have devised alludes to real American military projects like the High-frequency Active Auroral Research Program (HAARP), which has been blamed by conspiracy theorists for a variety of ills, ranging from climate control warfare to mass mind control to destructive earthquakes. Despite the country's strict isolation, North Koreans are evidently more than familiar with international conspiracy theories. *The Secret of Frequency A* is an example of the 'North Korea saves the world' genre of comic books, and it is no surprise that the nation

All Foreigners Look Alike!

An apocryphal story serves as an interesting counterpoint to the Western stereotype that all Asians look alike. (In Korea, this stereotype is extended to a real problem many Westerners have in remembering Korean names, because they are nearly all three syllables and so many Koreans have the surname Park, Kim or Lee.) In the early days after Korea's liberation from Japan, between 1945 and 1950, a Korean labourer was beaten to death by a Westerner in broad daylight in a public market in Seoul in front of hundreds of eyewitnesses. By the time the police arrived, the killer was long gone, but given the number of witnesses and the fact that he was a foreigner, police were confident that they could quickly find him. But they were terribly disappointed – and shocked – by the descriptions of the killer. All of the witnesses reported that he was tall and hairy, with a long nose and round eyes (some also reported that he smelled of spoiled milk) – the generic Korean stereotype of a foreign white man. When shown photos and asked whether they would be able to identify the murderer in a lineup, the witnesses said the foreigners all looked alike and they could not distinguish between them.

rescued by the child scientists is located in Africa, where the North Korean state has had ties for decades through their arms dealing.

Another North Korean comic book set in an unnamed African country is *Blizzard in the Jungle* (2001), a thriller aimed at an older readership of teens and adults. The two heroes of *Blizzard in the Jungle* are North Korean doctors whose surnames are both Kim, making them stand-ins for Kim Il-sung and Kim Jong-il. They are cast as the rescuers of a multiracial group that has survived a sabotage-induced plane crash atop a remote mountain. The survivors elect one of the Kims as their leader for his wisdom and virtuous qualities. He directs them in what appears to be a doomed endeavour – to climb *up* the mountain for rescue instead of going down, contrary to the apparent common sense of the rude and abrasive Americans in the group. In the end, Kim's strategy – symbolic of ascending North Korea's Mount Paektu, the mythic birthplace of his 'Eternal Leader' – turns out to be the better plan. The foolish Americans who abandon the group (because they have freedom of choice, after all, and decide to go with information they saw on TV) meet an appropriately gruesome fate as they are devoured by crocodiles in the valley.

The heroes in *Blizzard in the Jungle* have many occasions to repeat kernels of North Korean wisdom and strike several dramatic poses that mirror those of Kim Il-sung in statues and paintings familiar to all North Koreans. The Kims are characterized as the wise, open-minded, benevolent and compassionate saviours of an unnamed African people oppressed by what seems to be the American 'Mafia'.

The fact that North Korea is producing politically charged comics set in Africa reflects a political reality. After signing a protocol on negotiation and cooperation in 2013, North Korea supplied the Kabila regime of the Democratic Republic of Congo with troops and advisors in exchange for access to the uranium mines that had been a source of uranium for the first American atomic bomb. North Korean military advisors have also been active in Angola, Zimbabwe, Zambia, Ethiopia and Uganda, where they ran training camps and oversaw the use of heavy weapons imported from North Korea. What is surprising is that so much of North Korea's political strategy can be inferred from their comic books. But that may be because the *geurimchaek* are designed to be easily understood and are thereby more transparent than propaganda aimed only at adults.

Ironically, one of the best descriptions of North Korea to appear before the flood of YouTube videos in recent years was a comic book, *Pyongyang: A Journey in North Korea* (2003). The Canadian Québécois cartoonist, Guy Delisle, had spent two months working in the capital as an animator. Even films and photos do not come close to conveying the sense of scale or the emptiness of Pyongyang, which Delisle's greyscale graphic memoir so effectively evokes.

Kim Seondal: The Trickster Hero

One of the most popular folkloric figures to be found in North Korean comics is the nineteenth-century trickster figure Kim Seondal (김선달), also known as Bongi Kim Seondal (봉이김선달) in South Korea. The name Seondal is actually a reference to someone who has passed the civil service examination but has not yet been given a government post, so even Kim's name itself hints at being satirical, since to pass the exam but lack a position would be a disappointment. *Bong* means 'dupe', 'one who dupes', or 'a peak', so Bongi is read as 'trickster' while also being associated with someone of high status. What Kim Seondal usually does is dupe the wealthy people of the upper class by appealing to their greed and vanity.

In the best-known Kim Seondal story he sells the Taedong River, which flows through Pyongyang. He begins by distributing coins to the local peasants and paying them to return the money to him every time they draw water. The following day, a greedy *yangban* (aristocrat) sees Kim sitting at the riverbank collecting money. When he asks Kim why people are paying him, Kim explains that he owns the river and he is being paid for the water. He convinces the *yangban* of the easy fortune to be made and sells him title to the river for a huge sum. The next day, when the *yangban* comes to collect his money from the peasants, no one pays him, telling him he is crazy and that the water of the river is free for anyone to use.

In South Korea, Kim is a self-interested conman who serves to expose the hypocrisy and greed of the *yangban* class, often for something as small as a free meal. But in the North, he has been elevated to the status of a national folk hero because he is said to have come from Pyongyang, North Korea's capital, and his surname is Kim, linking him to the Kim dynasty. In modern North Korean tellings of the Kim Seondal stories, he is a hard worker who comes to the rescue of villagers and swindles the *yangban*, who are eager to make a profit by exploiting the rural peasants. He is the protector of local resources and sends the humiliated *yangban* packing from the countryside back to the big city.

In spite of his differing reputations in North and South, Kim is immensely popular in both Koreas. Several North Korean graphic novels feature him, including *The Disgrace of the Yangban Seongcheon* (2006), which tells four popular tales. In South Korea, he was the subject of *Seondal: The Man Who Sells the River* (2016), a film directed by Park Dae-min.

6

KOREA IN THE MODERN ERA

The pursuit of technological innovation is a hallmark of South Korea, which boasts one of the highest rates of internet connectivity and smartphone usage globally. Advancements in technology, including the development of 5G networks, robots and artificial intelligence, have positioned South Korea at the forefront of what is now called the Fourth Industrial Revolution. However, South Korea also faces its share of challenges, such as an ageing population, high levels of stress in both the workplace and education, and ongoing tensions with North Korea. South Korea currently has the lowest birth rate and the highest suicide rate among the thirty-seven countries that constitute the Organization for Economic Cooperation and Development, and many young Koreans say they are living in 'Hell Joseon'.

Despite its modern façade and the fact that it is one of the most wired countries on the planet – with all the problems that come with it – South Korea remains deeply rooted in tradition. Confucian principles, which have influenced Korean society for centuries, continue to shape interpersonal relationships, family dynamics, societal expectations and even corporate culture. The juxtaposition of modern skyscrapers against ancient palaces and temples in Seoul reflects both harmonious coexistence between and a clash of the old and the new. Traditional ceremonies, such as the Lunar New Year (*Seollal*, 설날) and harvest festival (*Chuseok*, 추석),

are still widely celebrated, connecting the people to their cultural heritage, while imported holidays like Christmas, Valentine's Day and, most recently, Halloween have made their way onto the annual calendar. Contemporary Korea is a dynamic blend of tradition and modernity, where the legacy of the past resonates alongside the ever-increasing pace of change, resulting in a society and culture under tremendous stress. The nation's journey from the ashes of war to economic prosperity and global cultural influence in the twenty-first century is both a testament to and test of its resilience and adaptability. Korea's modern narrative carries with it its history, folklore and origin stories, and like all such narratives, it is layered, with a surface that often belies underlying contradictions, and Koreans continue to create myths, legends and folk tales even while the means of communicating them have been transformed by technology.

THE MYTH OF DEMOCRACY

Textbooks will generally say that South Korea has been a democracy since 1948, but the truth is more complicated. The first 'democratic' president of South Korea, Syngman Rhee, was appointed by the Americans following the Second World War, and during his authoritarian administration the government was involved in two large-scale massacres: the suppression of the Jeju Island Uprising, which began in April of 1948 and lasted more than a year, leaving more than 20,000 dead; and the Bodo League Massacre, the mass execution of more than 100,000 Communist-sympathizing political prisoners at the outbreak of the Korean War. The election of 1960, which Rhee won uncontested, is generally considered to have been fraudulent. Rhee had charged one of his opponents, Cho Bong-am, the leader of the Progressive Party, with being a Communist. Cho was later tried and executed in what is now considered Korea's first 'judicial murder'. His other opponent, Cho Pyong-ok, leader of the Democratic Party, died of coronary thrombosis at the Walter Reed Army Medical Center in Washington, DC., where he was being treated for stomach cancer. These events, Rhee's evident intention to stay in power for life, and the murder of a student demonstrator who had protested against the rigged election, led to the widespread April Revolution in 1960, which Rhee violently suppressed, killing nearly 200 protesters. Rhee resigned afterwards and had to be secretly exfiltrated by the CIA. He died in exile in Hawaii.

Park Chung-hee, a former general who came to power through a coup d'état in 1961, ruled South Korea until 1979. His administration is responsible for South Korea's phenomenal economic growth – it was under his rule that South Korea's standard of living finally outstripped the North – but at the cost of intense political repression. During Park's administration, the Korean Central Intelligence Agency (KCIA, modelled on the American CIA) became a formidable force, and his army became an ally of the United States in the Vietnam War, quickly developing a reputation for its corruption and brutality towards the Vietnamese. Park survived two assassination attempts, though his wife was killed in one of them. In 1972, because of national dissent following rigged elections, he dissolved the National Assembly, declared martial law and suspended the constitution. Park then ruled as a dictator until October of 1979, when he was assassinated by his close friend, the director of the KCIA. This was followed, after an interim government that lasted only six days, by the December 12th Military Insurrection, another coup d'état by which General Chun Doo-hwan took power.

Chun Doo-hwan was then elected president by the Electoral College as a sole candidate and ruled between 1980 and 1988. The day after he took power under martial law, there were widespread student demonstrations in the city of Gwangju, during which protesters were beaten, tortured, raped and killed. This led to a city-wide uprising, which was violently suppressed by the Korean military over the next several days, resulting in the massacre of more than 2,000 civilians by some estimates. The Gwangju Uprising, as it is known, was a major turning point in South Koreans' attitude towards the United States. South Koreans – particularly those who had lived through the Korean War – had been almost uniformly pro-American until that point, but after the Gwangju Uprising, Americans were seen as complicit in the violent reprisals against the people of the city. Many Koreans felt betrayed because the US military had not intervened after repeated pleas for assistance in the name of democracy. South Korea's relations with the North also deteriorated, and in 1983, Chun narrowly survived an attempted assassination by North Korean agents that killed seventeen members of his entourage, including members of his cabinet, while he was visiting Yangon in Myanmar.

In 1987, after months of violent riots, Chun Doo-hwan agreed to step down, unexpectedly abiding by the term limit of seven years that had been established by his own 1981 constitution. That period in 1987–88 is generally cited as Korea's peaceful transition to democracy via the first democratic election, though it was hardly peaceful or even satisfactory for the public, given the riots that continued after the election of Ro Tae-woo. Ro was a former army general who had been hand-picked by Chun to be his successor and he would serve until 1993.

Korea's next democratically elected president, Kim Young-sam, who served between 1993 and 1998, would mount a strenuous anti-corruption campaign. Both former presidents Chun Doo-hwan and Ro Tae-woo were convicted of treason, mutiny and corruption. In 1995, Ro had attempted a preemptive public apology for having received hundreds of millions of dollars in secret political dona-tions during his time as president, but he was still charged. Together, Ro and Chun were fined more than $400 million. Ro was given a 22.5-year sentence (later commuted to 17 years). Chun was sen-tenced to death by hanging, but that was later commuted to life in prison. He paid only part of his fine, famously claiming, 'I have only 290,000 won to my name'. Chun would follow the ancient tradition of internal exile and spend two years at a Buddhist temple, living in a small, unheated room with his wife.

During Kim Young-sam's administration, the government also instituted a strong campaign of internationalization – termed *segyehwa* – but that was unfortunately overshadowed by the trials of his two predecessors. In December of 1997, on the advice of president-elect Kim Dae-jung, Kim Young-sam pardoned both Chun and Ro in the name of national reconciliation.

Kim Dae-jung had formerly survived an assassination attempt by Park Chung-hee and had been kidnapped and tortured by the KCIA. He had also been imprisoned and sentenced to death by Chun for allegedly fomenting the Gwangju Uprising, and both Chun and Ro had tried to have him killed. And yet when Kim became president in 1998, he would invite the two disgraced former presidents to the Blue House (Korea's 'White House') to ask their advice on political matters. Kim won the Nobel Peace Prize in 2000 for enacting the Sunshine Policy, thereby improving political and economic relations with a North Korea that had become increasingly volatile. Ironically, the policy got its name from 'The North Wind and the Sun', an Aesop's fable in which the two compete to see who is stronger. In the story, the gentle warmth of the Sun defeats the harsh cold of the North Wind, and Kim's naming of the policy implies that South Korea is the Sun and North Korea is the North Wind, implicitly critiquing the North Korean view that their Eternal Leader, Kim Il-sung, is the sun.

The above is just some of the political history of South Korea after the Korean War on a peninsula already divided after having just emerged from under the yoke of nearly half a century of colonization and attempted cultural eradication by the Japanese. Caught between neighbouring superpowers – a condition that had once earned it the appellation 'a shrimp caught between whales' – Korea had plenty of its own internal conflicts even in the face of having to deal with foreign interests and influences. The country hardly seemed capable of becoming a global superpower itself – but it did, and the evidence can be seen in the phenomenon of Hallyu.

THE K-WAVE: HALLYU ONSCREEN

Hallyu, written *hanryu* (한류/韓流), is a term originally coined by the Chinese media. It literally means 'Korean flow', referring to the flow of Korean media into China. The term quickly caught on, and came to refer more generally to what is now called the 'Korean Wave' or 'K-Wave' – the phenomenon of South Korean pop culture and its massive global popularity.

According to Korean scholars, the Hallyu phenomenon has its origins in the early 1990s, when the director of the Korean Overseas Information Service sneaked videotapes of the TV drama *What is Love* to the Korean consulate in Hong Kong via diplomatic pouch. The show was broadcast in Hong Kong and mainland China, reaching more than 50 million viewers, and it quickly became so popular that city streets emptied on the evenings when it aired.

Within just a few years, Korean TV dramas were playing in the Philippines, Vietnam, Malaysia, Taiwan and Japan, before spreading to Europe, South Asia, the Middle East and Latin America, including Cuba. There is a long list of popular K-dramas, but they may be best characterized by the qualities of *Winter Sonata* (2002), the first Korean breakthrough hit in Japan, which propelled its male lead, Bae Yong-joon, to such fame that the Japanese prime minister promised in his re-election bid in 2004 to try hard to be as popular as the Korean star. (When Bae Yong-joon visited Japan that year, 350 policemen had to be stationed at the airport to protect him from the mob of more than 3,000 women who had come to greet him.)

Winter Sonata is a romantic soap opera about the recovery of an innocent childhood romance in later years that features the classic amnesia trope, a tearjerker with an emphasis on the themes of nostalgia, heartbreak and recovery. Its protagonist is a brilliant young man who also happens to be introverted, socially awkward and emotionally sensitive, making him appeal particularly to Asian women. *Winter Sonata* was not only successful as a TV show, but was also responsible for creating an Asia-wide fashion trend and a surge in tourism to Korea, accounting for a reported $27 billion in total revenue.

These two early successes depicted clashing values in contemporary times – a theme resonant to all viewers in the Pacific Rim. *What is Love* features two multigenerational families, one conservative and one progressive, following the drama in their lives through fifty-five episodes. The storylines highlight the dilemma of maintaining traditional Confucian values while dealing with the pressures of global capitalism and its unremitting demand for status and success. *Winter Sonata* likewise inverts the typical ideal of the Confucian man, making its male protagonist especially attractive to middle-aged women, who would have most suffered under the double burden of Confucian patriarchy and rapid modernization.

The K-dramas and films that followed have expanded into just about every genre: zombies (*Train to Busan*, 2016), monsters (*The Host*, 2006), vampires (*Thirst*, 2009), science fiction (*Snowpiercer*, 2013), action (*The Man from Nowhere*, 2010), Asian Western (*The Good, the Bad, the Weird*, 2008), horror (*The Wailing*, 2016), and even successful remakes like *The Villainess* (2017), which amplifies the action and cinematography of the French film *La Femme Nikita* (1990) to a frenetic degree. The quality of Korean film has steadily improved both in production values and writing, keeping up with and at times surpassing the international competition.

In recent years, it has been impossible not to notice the global prominence of Korean cinema. In 2019, Bong Joon-ho's *Parasite*, which followed his successes with *The Host* and *Snowpiercer*, was not only the first Korean film to win the Palme d'Or at the Cannes, but also had the unprecedented honour of winning Best Picture, Director, Original Screenplay and International Feature Film at the 92nd American Academy Awards. It was the first foreign-language film to win an Oscar for Best Picture. Afterwards, *Parasite* went on to major rescreenings and a commercial success the Associated Press called the biggest 'Oscar effect' since *Gladiator* had won Best Picture in 2001.

Parasite's central themes – social stratification, poverty, exploitation of the poor, the arrogance of the affluent and the explosive release of social resentment – resonated with audiences throughout the world because they address universal concerns in modern society. These themes are also addressed, though in a more poignant and understated way, with a more psychological than allegorical tone, in Lee Chang-dong's *Burning* (2018), which had won the Fipresci International Critics' Prize at Cannes the year before. Bong and Lee's films served as the precursor to an even larger international phenomenon, Hwang Dong-hyuk's nine-episode TV series *Squid Game*, a brilliant collage of media satire, nostalgia and deep social criticism that ironically succeeds via the same medium it critiques.

Squid Game was the most watched Netflix show of all time in ninety-four countries in 2021. Part of its near universal appeal came from the fact that it was about financial desperation, suffering and nostalgia for an idealized past – all features that critiqued corporate capitalism. For Koreans, the story was especially poignant because it drew on memories of old childhood games, most of which had become obscure, replaced by video games after the influx of technology and rapid urbanization. To have those images then twisted into the basis of sadistic lethal contests that exploited financial desperation and greed struck a national chord. *Squid Game* was allegorical on the one hand but also verged on realism, and its spectacular international success only reiterated how South Korea's current social and economic conditions resonate with the rest of the world.

Every one of these films and TV shows can be seen as an example of the Korean penchant for syncretism and the culture's ability to assimilate and adapt foreign influences. Koreans have been cinephiles since the Japanese colonial era, and movie theatres sprang up everywhere in the post-war years. They began to show subtitled foreign films, many of which came via the US military, and even with the government censorship of foreign films, Koreans were exposed to a steady stream of American and European popular culture. Genre films like Spaghetti Westerns, horror films, American monster movies, vampire movies (particularly the British Hammer

A Joseon-era painting of a group of men playing the strategy board game *baduk*, also known as *go*.

Korea Arrives at Cannes

The Cannes Film Festival, founded in 1946 and held annually in the spring, is considered the most prestigious film festival in the world. It is not only a glamorous media frenzy, but also a highly selective competition overseen by a discerning jury that emphasizes artistic merit. Some of the most iconic films of all time have premiered there – even being selected for Cannes can be a career-changing event in the life of a film-maker. The festival also hosts the Marché du Film, the world's largest film market, at which distributors buy and sell films, and so recognition at Cannes is an honour that can not only provide global publicity but also prove to be financially lucrative.

Korea did not gain significant recognition from Cannes until the twenty-first century, when Hallyu became the force to contend with that it remains to this day.

2002 Im Kwon-taek's 98th film, *Painted Fire*, is co-winner for Best Director – the first Korean film to win an award at Cannes.

2004 Park Chan-wook's violent revenge film *Oldboy* wins the Grand Prix.

2007 Jeon Do-yeon wins Best Actress in Lee Chang-dong's film, *Secret Sunshine*. She is only the second Asian actress to receive the award.

2010 Lee Chang-dong's *Poetry* wins Best Screenplay and Hong Sang-soo's *Hahaha* wins the Un Certain Regard Prize.

2011 Kim Ki-duk's documentary *Arirang* is co-winner of the Un Certain Regard Prize.

2013 Moon Byoung-gon's short film *Safe* wins the Palme d'Or.

2018 Lee Chang-dong's *Burning* wins the Fipresci International Critics' Prize.

2019 Bong Joon-ho's *Parasite* wins the Grand Prix by unanimous decision.

2022 Park Chan-wook wins Best Director for *Decision to Leave* and Song Kang-ho wins Best Actor (only the third Asian actor to receive the award) for his role in *Broker*, a Korean film directed by the Japanese director Hirokazu Kore-eda.

films starring Chrisopher Lee), MGM musicals and James Bond movies, and eventually a steady stream of Hollywood blockbusters, were dominating the Korean screens and bringing in the majority of revenue. This was seen as both an economic and cultural problem even before terms like 'cultural imperialism' came into use for the incursion of foreign – and especially American – content into other popular media like music and television. Remedying this problem, which concerned artists, academics and the government alike (particularly following the change in Korea's political climate after the Gwangju Uprising in the mid-1980s), was one of the underlying motivating forces behind what eventually became the Hallyu phenomenon. Koreans felt they should no longer be only the recipients of outside cultural influences, but the creators of their own culture.

With the K-Wave, Korea has turned the issue of cultural production around into a more complex feedback loop. Its expression of 'soft power' has even led to charges of cultural imperialism by other countries. But the global success of Korean film can also be seen as a demonstration of the Koreans' unique ability to imbue their dramas with their own traditions, made all the more powerful for the deeply resonating sense of *han*.

Han (한 / 恨) is a complex and nuanced concept in Korean culture, often described as a mixture of sorrow, resentment, grief, regret and anger that accumulates over time and is passed down through generations. It is not just a fleeting emotion, but said to be an enduring weight carried in the hearts of the Korean people. Those who die with the burden of their *han* unrelieved are said to become unhappy ghosts. *Han* is described as a heavy, unresolved and lingering emotion that is not easily expressed or alleviated. It can be personal, focusing on individual experiences of loss and suffering, or

The Myth of *Han*

These days, *han* is generally considered a unique element of the Korean national character, to the degree that some non-Koreans erroneously believe that the name for Korea, *Hanguk*, means 'Nation of *Han*'. The *han* in *Hanguk* (韓) is actually a name character referring to the Korean nation after the fall of Joseon. The current understanding of *han* did not, in fact, become prevalent until the Japanese colonial era, and it is intellectuals and writers from that period who shaped the concept into what it is now, perhaps as a response to Japan's attempts to eradicate Korean identity. When it is used in older Korean texts, it tends to be associated with personal grief or loss rather than the accumulated bitterness and collective historical weight associated with the contemporary concept. Some scholars argue that the contemporary idea of *han* is an 'invented tradition', but tradition is a constantly evolving phenomenon and it is more accurate to say that *han* has evolved over time in keeping with historical conditions.

collective, reflecting the shared history of pain and trauma endured by the Korean people. It can manifest in various ways, from melancholic resignation to fierce indignation, deep depression to violent anger, or as a yearning and a struggle to find justice after being wronged. The term itself rarely appears in classical Korean literature, but given Korea's turbulent history marked by repeated foreign invasions, colonization, internal strife, class conflict and the legacy of the Korean War, it is no wonder that the idea of *han* would seem to be a cultural legacy handed down from ancient times.

The concept of *han* is expressed in Korean literature, music, art and film. In contemporary TV dramas and movies, it is often an underlying theme or a motivation that propels the plot (most explicitly in ghost stories and horror stories) and imparts an especially poignant, tragic tone. It is also often retroactively injected into old folk tales in their retelling in order to highlight tragic themes. For example, in modern versions of the story of Arang (see p. 143), the storyteller might emphasize the fact that the solving of her murder relieved her *han* and permitted her ghost to move on to the next world.

Perhaps the best example of Korean film-makers' ability to weave global influences in with their own cultural traditions is a lesser-known film from 2003, Jang Joon-hwan's frenetic meta-genre-bending *Save the Green Planet!* Jang's film won the Korean Film Award for Best New Director and the Best of Bucheon award at the Bucheon International Fantastic Film Festival, as well as Best Film and Best New Director at the Busan Film Critics Awards – all in Korea. Yet *Save the Green Planet!* was a total disaster at the box office, with initial returns of under $16,000 on its $3-million production budget. Some even said Jang should not have released the film on 4 April (4/4), an inauspicious date comprised of two number fours (*sa*/사), which sounds like 'death' in Korean. But the central problem was probably that the film's posters and promotion had made it appear to be a romantic comedy, and initial audiences were stunned, baffled, horrified and disappointed, not appreciating its depth and complexity.

Save the Green Planet! is a truly international film, and its many layers of meaning practically require a degree in film studies to decipher. In interviews, Jang mentioned two primary influences: the film adaptation of Stephen King's novel *Misery* (1987), and the internet rumour that Leonardo DiCaprio was an alien. These sub-texts are apparent in the movie, but it is also a running sequence of allusions, both subtle and obvious, to foreign influences and to the domestic effect of foreign influences. What follows is only a small selection of the most apparent.

The opening theme music is 'Somewhere Over the Rainbow', a reference to the Technicolor classic *The Wizard of Oz* (1939). The cassette tape is inserted into a car's sound system, which evoke's the car chase in Luc Besson's 1985 thriller *Subway*. The suspected alien in the film is held captive in a cluttered basement room reminiscent of a scene in Ridley Scott's 1982 sci-fi epic *Blade Runner*. The protagonist is a beekeeper, referring to Sherlock Holmes. The protagonist's tightrope-walker girlfriend is a nod to the French/Italian comedy-drama *King of Hearts* (1966), and his dog is an allusion to Toto, again from *The Wizard of Oz*. There is a grungy and eccentric detective, evoking Columbo, and when the kidnapping is solved, we see a montage that contains references to Brian Singer's *The Usual Suspects* (1995) and Stanley Kubrick's *2001: A Space Odyssey* (1968). The apocalyptic ending of the movie evokes *The Hitchhiker's Guide to the Galaxy* (2005), John Carpenter's *Dark Star* (1974), and even the drooling aliens from *The Simpsons*. And yet *Save the Green Planet!* is also a deeply sentimental and political film showing the legacy of the Korean government's violent crackdown on the labour protests of the 1980s and the consequences of worker exploitation by Korea's corporate powers – those allusions being apparent to everyone in the Korean audience. The film is ultraviolent and satirical by turns, and the story itself does not conclude until the very end, when a broken television set appears in the poignant end credits.

Save the Green Planet! is a film whose origin is in the expression of *han*, which also performs its own drama through a series of foreign incursions – the majority of them undetected by the typical Korean viewer – and it offers a profound critique of Korea's economy, politics and culture, extending that message to the entire world. In that sense, Jang's film shares the qualities of classical Korean literature, which used to be written in Chinese with layered allusions to the Chinese classics and thus could only be appreciated by the educated elite. Despite its domestic box office failure, *Save the Green Planet!* has developed an international cult following and may prove to be the enduring sleeper of the Hallyu phenomenon.

Hallyu has also produced what appears to be a continuing stream of more accessible films and TV series that highlight Korean history, mythology and folk tradition. The continuing appeal of the fox-demon figure from folklore can be seen not only in fantasy series like

Reimagining the Past

One of the best examples of contemporary mythifying in Korea is the transformation of production values in historical films and TV dramas. In the years following the Korean War and into the late 1970s, historical films tended to rely on extant settings and inexpensive costumes. The result was that the typical historical drama looked cheap and sparse, with a minimum of material culture in the background. This sparseness was exacerbated by the fact that much of Korea's landscape, particularly forests, were still recovering from the devastation caused by the bombings during the war years. The result was that the typical Korean's imagination of Korea's past was somewhat bleak.

Following the 'economic miracle' years, as Korea approached the twenty-first century, Korean studios could devote bigger budgets as well as better technology to film production. The result was far better production values that permitted depictions of a more vivid and epic past. To a contemporary Korean, those older historical representations feel impoverished and do not hold up to the newly imagined visions of Korea's more opulent history, even while the narratives themselves might be tragic.

Hometown Legends (2008), but also in romantic comedies, like *My Girlfriend is a Gumiho* (2010), and the drama *Tale of the Nine Tailed* (2010). Epic historical movies, like *The Fortress* (2017), seem to have merged with the imported zombie genre to create internationally popular Netflix series like *Kingdom* (2019), in which zombies are projected back into the Joseon era. The American hit film *The Sixth Sense* (1999) seems to have inspired numerous TV dramas in which detectives, policemen and others 'see dead people', though usually in a uniquely Korean tragicomic way, and allusions to the Taoist/Buddhist Hells, especially appealing to Chinese audiences, make their appearance in films like *Together with God: Sin and Punishment* (2017).

Hallyu, particularly following COVID, has served to increase and diversify viewerships in Korea, and some TV series take the opportunity to educate both the domestic and foreign audience about Korean history and culture. *Secret Royal Inspector & Joy* (2001), for instance, makes regular use of on-screen footnotes to explain archaic terms and customs even while it includes nods to foreign influences – the first episode uses theme music reminiscent of a Spaghetti Western, both highlighting and poking fun at the fact that the Secret Royal Inspector wears a black horsehair hat (the traditional *gat*) as if he were a gunslinger. This kind of self-conscious international humour also appears in shows like the comedy detective drama *Behind Your Touch* (2023). Its original title was *Hiphagae*, or literally 'Hiply', referring to the protagonist, a veterinarian who can communicate with pets by holding their hips. One of the other characters in the show is a queer-coded male shaman who is possessed by the spirit of the 'Great General' – not the traditional Korean spirit, but that of American military commander Douglas MacArthur, who played a major role in the Pacific Theatre in the Second World War and is often characterized as

Two men wearing the traditional *gat*,
a lightweight hat woven out of horsehair.

Korea's saviour. The shaman's nickname is 'Five Star', which alludes not only to the 'Seven Stars' familiar in shaman shrines but also to the number of stars in MacArthur's military rank.

HALLYU DIPLOMACY

One of the unexpected functions of K-Drama and film are their role in North–South diplomacy. To an outside viewer, this may simply seem to be the product of creativity and marketing, because films and TV shows with North–South themes tend to be popular. But government influence should not be overlooked. South Korean official policy regarding North Korea has gone through a radical change in recent decades. In the years after the Korean War and up until the end of the Chun Doo-hwan administration in 1988, South Korean school textbooks were full of anti-Communist propaganda with uniformly negative depictions of the North. But after democratization the government attitude, no longer dominated by a militaristic Cold War culture, became markedly more favourable in its representations of North Korea.

For example, refugees from North Korea, once called 'defectors', are now called 'emigres'. Elementary and middle-school textbooks no longer heavily emphasize an imminent threat of invasion from North Korea. There is a concerted deconstruction of North Korea's own propaganda and mythmaking, but there is also an intense scrutiny of media representations of North Korea coming from foreign sources. The nuclear threat posed by North Korea is undeniably real, as Kim Jong-un regularly demonstrates, but South Korea's dealings with the North have become more nuanced. This change in attitude has resulted in new positive stereotypes of North Koreans, expressed in films and TV dramas that show cooperation and sympathy between North and South, from military- and espionage-themed films to romantic comedies.

The first prominent film in this category was the tragic thriller-romance titled *Shiri* (1999) in foreign release, which focuses on a female North Korean assassin and a male South Korean investigator. At the time of its release, *Shiri* had the highest production budget of any South Korean film and broke domestic box-office records, as well as becoming a top-grossing film in Hong Kong. The film's title – *Swiri* (쉬리) in Korean – is symbolic of the complex relationship between North and South. A *swiri* (*Coreoleuciscus splendidus*, or 'Splendid Korean Dance') is a species of fish found in the rivers of both parts of the Korean peninsula, unaware of whether it swims in Communist or democratic waters.

In 2000, *JSA: Joint Security Area*, directed by Park Chan-wook (who would go on to achieve international fame with *Oldboy*), became the highest-grossing film in Korean history. *JSA* is a military procedural about a bilateral investigation into the killing of two North Korean soldiers in the Joint Security Area, and it addresses the political and moral issues that imbue the tragedy of North and South Korean soldiers becoming close friends in the DMZ.

JSA was followed by numerous other films and TV series: *Spy Girl* (2004), a light-hearted *Shiri*; *Iris* (2009), a spinoff of *Shiri*; *Confidential Assignment* (2017), a buddy cop film in which the North Korean is a model of virtue and competence while the bumbling South Korean provides the comic relief; *Secretly Greatly* (2013), an 'action comedy-drama' in which three North Korean sleeper agents go undercover in the South as a rock musician, a high school student and a village idiot; *Red Family* (2013), a more serious film about sleeper agents whose mission is to kill North Korean defectors (directed by Kim Ki-duk, who had won the Un Certain Regard Prize at Cannes in 2011 for his documentary *Arirang*); *Steel Rain* (2017), a bold thriller in which South Koreans help to prevent a coup d'état in the North, rescue the Supreme Leader, and return him to power in exchange for half of their nuclear arsenal; *Crash Landing on You* (2019), a romantic comedy series that applies a Romeo & Juliet theme to a young female South Korean CEO and a North Korean army captain who is from an elite family; and *Confidential Assignment 2* (2022), this time featuring a Korean American FBI agent in the international mix.

Of the above films and TV dramas, which is only a select list, the most interesting and innovative when it comes to the theme of diplomacy is *Crash Landing on You*. The original Korean title, *Sarangui Bulsichak* (사랑의 불시착) literally translates 'Crash Landing of Love'. The show relies on the unusual and absurd premise that a successful female CEO – on the eve of inheriting her corrupt father's mega-corporation – could paraglide into a tornado in South Korea and end up in the DMZ, where she is then discovered by a captain of the People's Army, whose squad is on patrol there. The captain hides her in his home, which happens to be located in a quaint North Korean village modelled on the 'Peace Village' (see p. 176). Yet the village is not simply a charade designed to convey North Korean propaganda; instead, it ends up representing South Korean nostalgia about the 'good old days' before everything was taken over by cell phones, the internet, and Western consumer goods. The South Korean woman learns a great deal about simple traditional community virtues even while masquerading as the captain's fiancée and knowing that she is in mortal danger.

Poster for the 2000 film
JSA: Joint Security Area.

Crash Landing on You shows the corruption of both South Korean corporations and the North Korean military, the villains of each side sharing the common motivations of money and power. The female and male protagonists, on the other hand, represent the 'good' aspects of capitalism and communism. By presenting a clean and sanitized version of North Korean daily life to South Korean viewers and dramatizing how traditional Korean notions of virtue can exist even in communism, *Crash Landing on You* does a remarkable job of conveying implicit political messages to both sides. The producers of the show not only relied on North Korean emigres for authentic details, they also clearly knew that the show would be smuggled into North Korea and be seen by both the privileged class and those in rural areas (even at the risk of their lives).

THE DOUBLE EDGE OF K-POP

Another major facet of Hallyu – and perhaps even more prominent on the world stage than its films and dramas – is K-pop, with its army of beautiful idols and millions upon millions of worshipping fans. The sea change in the international engagement with K-pop was prompted by PSY's 2012 'Gangnam Style', the first YouTube video to get more than a billion views (and more than 5 billion by January 2024). But PSY, with his combination of parody, satire and wild humour, is actually atypical for the genre. The artist most closely foreshadowing the current style of K-pop is perhaps Rain, who came to pan-Asian prominence in the early 2000s and would go on to act in Hollywood films. But the trajectory of K-pop can be traced back to the impoverished post-Korean War years and the emergence of groups like the Kim Sisters, who began their careers by performing for American GIs.

The Kim Sisters (one of them actually an adopted cousin) would become regulars on *The Ed Sullivan Show*, the longest-running variety show in history, singing covers of well-known songs in their noticeably accented English. Their mother was a popular Korean singer. Their father, a composer who hit them if they made mistakes during their music lessons, was kidnapped and later executed in North Korea. Later in their career, the Kim Sisters were joined for a short time by the Kim Brothers, though they never became as popular. In the same period, the most internationally recognized solo singer from Korea was Patti Kim (Kim Hye-ja), who had also begun her career performing for American soldiers and would go on to appear in Las Vegas, at Carnegie Hall and on *The Johnny Carson Show*.

Well into the 1980s, South Korea was still under oppressive rule and its media heavily censored. While these social and economic conditions were not conducive to the development of an indigenous musical tradition parallel to America's rock and roll, innovative bands did emerge, their music and performance dovetailing with the student anti-government movements of the late 1970s and into the late 1980s. The most prominent of these appeared in the early 1990s: Seo Taiji and Boys, a group somewhat parallel to New York's Beastie Boys. Seo Taiji and Boys became a controversial national phenomenon for their social criticism, and for incorporating elements of heavy metal and rap culture in their music and public persona. Seo Taiji fused these foreign sounds with traditional Korean ballads and instruments, like the hourglass drum and the *piri*, a reed flute associated with classical Korean music, village festivals and Shamanic ceremonies. Seo Taiji disbanded in 1996, but by then they had made Koreans familiar with their kind of syncretic fusion of traditions. Producers could see the formation of a unique Korean pop sound, and recognized its potential international appeal. In fact, one of the band members, Yang Hyun-suk, would found YG Entertainment, one of Korea's largest media companies, establishing a direct lineage between the success of his former band and future K-pop artists. YG Entertainment would go on to produce 'Gangnam Style' as well as the girl group and global phenomenon Blackpink.

K-pop owes a great deal of its success to the business acumen of its producers, but as with Hallyu film and TV dramas, there was

Detail of a painting of guardian deities, Suguksa Temple, *c.* 1795. These are musicians playing traditional Korean instruments. The middle figure is playing the *janggu*, the hourglass drum.

also early involvement by members of the government. The phenomenal reception of K-pop groups in France was largely due to the behind-the-scenes promotional work of Choe Jun-ho, director of the Korean Cultural Center in Paris in the early 2000s. He obtained funding from the Korean government and approached producers, finally convincing SM Entertainment to send groups under their management. He also coordinated international press coverage and arranged newsworthy publicity events like the appearance of flash mobs in multiple cities in France demanding K-pop – a flash mob dancing in front of the glass pyramid at the Louvre made international headlines. In April of 2011, when tickets became available for the third SMTOWN Live World Tour, featuring five Korean bands (Girls' Generation, SHINee, Super Junior, f(x) and TVXQ), they sold out in the first fifteen minutes.

The nine-member girl group Twice won the *Billboard* Women in Music Breakthrough Artist Award in 2023, but the current global leaders in K-pop are Blackpink and BTS. Blackpink, the four-member girl group that debuted in 2016, are so important to the nation that South Korea's president, Moon Jae-in, praised them in 2021 for being leading figures in the promotion of Korean culture abroad. He pointed out how they were helping Korea become a 'cultural powerhouse' and promised future government support for groups like them. Blackpink made the cover of *TIME* magazine as Entertainers of the Year in 2022 and were invested as honorary MBEs (Members of the Order of the British Empire) by King Charles III in 2023. They are acknowledged by many publications as the biggest girl group in the world. The seven-member boy band BTS (short for the Bangtan Boys, or the Bulletproof Boyscouts) made the cover of *TIME* magazine in 2020 and is the most awarded musical group in

Traditional Korean instruments, featuring from left to right: a *bhuk*,
a *gayageum*, a *janggu* and a *kkwaenggwari*.

Korean history. According to the Bank of Korea, BTS was responsible for bringing in an additional $5 billion to the South Korean economy in 2021 by increasing tourism and creating a spill-over interest in all things Korean, including the Korean language. K-pop groups like Blackpink and BTS are directly responsible for the phenomenon of 'Koreaboos' – devoted fans who immerse themselves in Korean language and culture in order to be closer to their idols.

The term 'idol' (아이돌) – which comes from the Japanese *idoru*, an appropriation of the English 'idol' – is appropriate for the famous K-pop celebrities because they are not only objects of worship, but also, in a sense, false gods. An idol adored by fans is a carefully constructed and managed *persona* into which a production company has invested millions of dollars over the course of their rigorous contract, which may be for up to thirteen years. Everything about Korean pop idols, from their weight to their fashionable wardrobes, immaculate complexions and virtuous personalities, is monitored and controlled in order to encourage the creation of parasocial relationships, ultimately a source of revenue. Korean music managers and producers are generally men who have served in the military, and it comes as no surprise that the training regimen for K-pop stars involves harsh discipline that applies to nearly every aspect of life. The mental and physical burnout suffered by K-pop idols, leading to physical collapses from exhaustion onstage and even, in numerous high-profile cases, to suicide, are the consequences of maintaining the K-pop myth.

THE MYTH OF K-BEAUTY

One of the direct results of the K-Wave phenomenon is the fact that South Korea is currently the world's number one destination for 'medical tourism'. The Gangnam area of Seoul – made famous by PSY – is home to hundreds of clinics that specialize in cosmetic surgery, all located within a single square mile. As of 2021, medical tourism had brought more than three million visitors to the country. It is a major boost to South Korea's economy, and is supervised by the Ministry of Culture, Sports and Tourism, who issue warnings regarding 'ghost surgery', where a procedure is performed by an unqualified or unlicensed doctor rather than the one who interviewed the patient. In spite of this rampant practice, the industry is thriving, demand driven by images of Korean celebrities made prominent by the K-Wave. Ironically, two major media scandals contributed heavily to this tourism, reinforcing the myth that Korean doctors could make literally anyone look like a K-pop star or a beauty queen rather than exposing the risks of plastic surgery.

The 2012 Miss Korea pageant caused an uproar when the winner, Kim Yu-mi, was revealed to have undergone plastic surgery. 'Before'

The packaging for *Bakgabun*, the first mass-produced cosmetic item in Korea and a bestseller between 1915 and 1930.

and 'after' photos of her showing the degree to which her facial features had changed – violating her privacy – were posted prominently online. A major controversy was ignited, with accusations that she had cheated because the surgery had given her an unfair advantage (despite the fact that many other contestants had also undergone cosmetic procedures). Kim admitted to having surgery, but claimed that she had not misled anyone and that her 'inner beauty' should also be considered. Public opinion was divided, and while the controversy contributed to the international discussion regarding unrealistic standards for female beauty – highlighting the extremity of such pressures in Korea – it seems only to have amplified the problem.

A decade later, the Miss Korea pageant once again prompted an international scandal, this time for its 'cookie-cutter' finalists. Both critics and fans pointed out that all of the 2022 finalists had undergone plastic surgery to conform to an 'ideal' face type. Many viewers said the winner and the finalists were nearly indistinguishable, and just as in 2012, 'before' images of the contestants were tracked down and posted on the internet. While the 2022 scandal became somewhat of a national embarrassment, it also served as an advertisement for the skill of Korean plastic surgeons and contributed to a surge in medical tourism after the sudden decline caused by the COVID years.

The two pageant scandals show the profound resonance of Korea's Confucian culture, in particular the oppressive burden on women created by Confucian ideals and exacerbated by the influence of Western media. The myth that beauty and virtue go together is already perpetuated by classic folk tales and literature, as in the stories of Shimcheong and Chunhyang, and further amplified by an underlying cultural belief in physiognomy – certain facial proportions and shapes are said to reveal character traits like intelligence, honesty, loyalty and compassion, but when such standards are then combined with Western media ideals, the result can be a face whose appearance is unnatural and perhaps even uncanny. In fact, the 'ideal' Korean face now is the 'egg-shaped' face, which ironically resonates with the terrifying figure of the egg ghost.

The pressure to be attractive in order to get ahead in life and the prejudice directed towards those considered unattractive is called 'lookism', which also happens to be the title of a popular Korean webtoon published in 2014. The fact that plastic surgery also leads to intense unwanted scrutiny and criticism, violation of privacy, and even endangerment is yet another form of oppression women have to suffer in contemporary Korean society. South Korean girls from affluent families often face intense pressure to conform to such unrealistic standards, and in recent years it has become common for girls to get plastic surgery as a high-school graduation gift and even in middle school. It has also become a common practice to hire an investigator to track down a potential spouse's pre-surgery appearance (with the rationalization that it is a way to anticipate the appearance of one's children). The influence of domestic media and cosmetic firms, and especially television dramas, is so great that even some middle-aged men have begun to wear make-up and get plastic surgery and chemical peels.

HALLYU IN LITERATURE

It wasn't until 2011, when the English translation of Shin Kyung-sook's *Please Look After Mom* made the *New York Times* bestseller list, that Korean literature could be claimed as part of the Hallyu phenomenon. The novel, which sold more than a million copies in Korea during the first year of its publication in 2009 and won the Man Asia Literary Prize in 2011, addresses poignant themes and urgent contemporary social issues, namely the dissolution of the extended Confucian family structure and the plight of the elderly. The novel resonated deeply with Korean readers, who were exposed regularly to news stories about senior citizens with dementia being abandoned by their families. Written from the perspectives of multiple family members, *Please Look After Mom* examines the repercussions of a tragic accident: an elderly father becomes separated from his wife, who suffers from Alzheimer's disease, at a subway station. She is never found. The English translation was released on Mother's Day in the US, a marketing move that served to amplify its themes to Americans, who are in the midst of their own crisis with the elderly.

K-Wave in *The New Yorker*

The New Yorker is considered the most prestigious literary venue in the United States, having nurtured generations of great writers. The magazine's dedication to excellence has shaped American culture for the past century, and 2006 saw the publication of the first Korean literary works in *The New Yorker*: four poems by Ko Un, a Buddhist poet who had been imprisoned several times for his pro-democracy activism and was Korea's major hope for the Nobel Prize until his fall from grace due to charges that emerged from the #MeToo movement.

As of 2023, *The New Yorker* has published four pieces of fiction by major Korean writers: Yi Mun-yol's 'An Anonymous Island' (2011), told from a young wife's point of view, exposing the hypocrisy of the Confucian preoccupation with pure bloodlines; Pyun Hye-young's 'Caring for Plants' (2017), a dark story of a mother's vengeance against her son-in-law, who was responsible for her daughter's death; 'The Middle Voice' (2023), by Han Kang, which dwells on the issue of gender, language and identity; and 'Snowy Day', by Lee Chang-dong, director of *Burning* and other internationally acclaimed films, which dramatizes the tragic death of a young South Korean soldier near the DMZ.

Five years later, Han Kang's novel *The Vegetarian* – originally published in Korea in 2007 and then in English translation in 2015 in the UK and in 2016 in the US – won the Man Booker International Prize, and also made *TIME* magazine's list of best books. Like Shin's novel, it is written from multiple perspectives and explores dark themes, in this case women's identity in the face of oppressive Confucian patriarchy and the penchant for violence in Koreans' treatment of women. It also resonated deeply with the international readership and has been translated into twenty-three languages.

Bandi: North Korea's Hidden Voice

The name Bandi (반디) is a pseudonym that means 'firefly'. Because any information that could reveal his true identity would result in his execution and the incarceration of his relatives in prison camps, what follows from the introduction to Bandi's *The Red Years* – provided by Do Hee-yun, Representative of the Citizens' Coalition for Human Rights of Abductees and North Korean Refugees – is purposely minimal.

Bandi was born in North Korea in 1950 and was a member of the Chosun Writers' League Central Committee, meaning that he was an approved member of North Korea's literary elite, writing propaganda for the state. Most of his work in North Korean magazines was published in the 1970s. His politics changed when he witnessed the national trauma and the deaths of friends and colleagues during the Arduous March of the mid-1990s. Do writes of Bandi, 'The experiences of this time made him resolve to share with the outside world a true likeness of the harsh North Korean society as he himself saw it.' He did not escape North Korea, though he had the opportunity, because he feared for the safety of his family. Instead, his work – both prose and poetry that documents the everyday lives of North Koreans under an oppressive government – was smuggled out through China.

In 2017, seven of Bandi's short stories, in English translation, were published to international acclaim in a volume titled *The Accusation*. A volume of lyric poetry, *The Red Years*, followed in 2019. It is not certain whether Bandi is an individual or a group of writers, but the layers of symbolism contained in the pseudonym attest to the fact that Bandi is a highly trained and talented writer who has also carefully studied the mechanisms of propaganda. On its surface, *bandi* is a colloquial term for a firefly. But the first sylla-ble, *ban*, means 'half', and it results in many thematically relevant words with *ban* as a prefix. Bandi sounds similar to *bando* (반도) , meaning 'belt', which may symbolize not only the DMZ that divides the peninsula in half but also a leather belt used to beat people. *Bando* also means 'halfway' and 'peninsula'. Bandi also sounds like *bandae* (반대), which means 'the opposite' or 'to oppose', signify-ing a denouncement of the state, as well as recalling the beginning of the phrase *bandeusi* (반드시), which means 'right away', 'directly' and 'without fail'. One of the unexpected readings of the first sylla-ble comes from the Chinese character, 飯, which means 'food' or 'to eat', resonating with the theme of starvation during the great famine of the mid-1990s.

This intense layering of meanings is characteristic of a poetic writer, but also suggests the possibility that Bandi's identity was created by the dialogue of more than one individual. The layered meanings in the pseudonym are also a clue that Bandi's prose and poetry contain a similar dense encoding of meanings, used to reveal the oppression of the very state that trained him.

One of Bandi's most explicitly critical lyric poems is called 'Song of the Red People':

Great Leader, Great Leader,
you are the sky and we are just bugs.
Strike us down with your furious lightning,
but tell us, just tell us that you love us,
and if you heed this one small wish
there will be no thought of gnashing teeth.

Great Leader, Great Leader,
you are the whip – we are horse and oxen.
Ride us, beat us, to your heart's content,
just please, please, do not let us starve or freeze,
and if you heed this one small plea
we'll have no fleeting thought of crossing over.

Great Leader, Great Leader,
you're iron chains and we are slaves.
Rope us, bind us to your heart's content,
only, only, do not plug our eyes, ears, mouths,
for if you heed this small request
we shall never think to turn on you.

Bandi's current whereabouts is unknown. His work is banned in North Korea, and anyone found in possession of it could face the death penalty.

ARIRANG: THE REAL ANTHEM OF THE KOREAS

The traditional folk song 'Arirang' (아리랑) is deeply etched into the collective soul of Koreans. There are more than 3,600 variants of the song throughout the peninsula, with the number growing as more and more versions are posted online. Every province and even specific villages have their own variant of the song, which is sung at both sombre and festive gatherings. The *Aegukga* (애국가), or 'Patriotic Song' – whose melody was once based on 'Auld Lang Syne' – is the official national anthem of South Korea. North Korea's

Aegukga is a song usually called 'Shine Bright the Dawn', which is reminiscent of the national anthem of former East Germany. But 'Arirang' is considered, by many Koreans of both sides, to be the true national anthem of the Koreas. In fact, 'Arirang' was submitted for inclusion in the UNESCO Intangible Cultural Heritage list twice, once by each of the Koreas.

There are numerous theories about the origin of 'Arirang', but its true source remains a mystery. The more credible scholarship suggests that the song was first mentioned in a manuscript in 1756, and linguistic analysis suggests the term 'Arirang' is a combination of *ari* (아리), an ancient Korean term for 'long', and *ryeong* (령 / 嶺), which means 'mountain' and 'to lead'. That reading is in keeping with the lyrics, which describe going over a mountain pass:

Arirang, Arirang, Arariyo
Crossing over Arirang Pass
The dear one who abandons me
Shall not walk even ten *li* before going lame.

The song warns that the consequence of abandoning the speaker will be lameness – *balbyeong* (발병), literally, 'foot disease' or 'sore feet'. The song may also be linked to the legend of Princess Bari, the origin story for Korean shamans (see p. 65). Princess Bari's name sounds like a reference to 'feet,' and she was the 'abandoned one,' or Baridegi (바리데기), who brought curative medicine from a distant land beyond the mountains. Though its lyrics are about the possibility of abandonment and separation from a loved one, the song itself is often unifying when it is sung when families, friends and other groups are gathered together.

During the Japanese colonial era, 'Arirang' became a song of resistance, and it was sung at the March 1st Movement in 1919 to protest Japanese rule. After the Korean War, it was adopted by the 7th Infantry Division of the US Army as its official marching song. The best-known lyrics of 'Arirang' are the ones that were used in the lost 1926 film of the same name directed by Na Un-gyu, a tragic story about Koreans oppressed by the Japanese. It is said that entire teary-eyed audiences sang the song together while watching it. When Im Kwon-taek won the award for Best Director at Cannes in 2002, he recited 'Arirang' during his acceptance speech. A decade later, when Kim Ki-duk accepted the Golden Lion Award at the Venice Film Festival, he surprised everyone by singing 'Arirang' as his acceptance speech, though he had said he would sing the national anthem. Kim explained: 'Koreans sing when we are sad, when we feel alone, when we feel desperate, but also when we're happy.'

REUNIFICATION: IDEOLOGY, DREAM OR MYTH?

Reunification of the Korean peninsula has been hoped and planned for even before Korea was officially divided into North and South. Both North and South live with the tragic legacy of the war, which devastated the peninsula and left the scar of the DMZ as a constant reminder both of division and of the possibility of continued conflict, and since the armistice of 1953 both North and South have used the idea of reunification as a political and ideological tool. The North Korean policy of *Juche*, for example, implicitly includes the idea of Korea as a single, unified, self-reliant nation. In the South, the slogan *jayutongil* (자유 통일), literally 'free unification', is found on banners prominently displayed on every road approaching or leaving the DMZ area.

For the generation that remembers the Korean War firsthand, the dream of reunification is very real, because as many as ten million families were split during the conflict. Some were permanently separated by the DMZ, while others lost track of each other in the chaos of war. In 1983, a live TV show called *Finding Dispersed Families* aired on the Korean Broadcasting System as part of a nationwide initiative to reunite families that had been scattered by the war. Thousands of tearful people gathered with placards listing the names of their relatives along with identifying details. The live broadcast began on 30 June – five days after the 30th anniversary of the outbreak of the Korean War – and continued until 14 November. It had been intended to run for only 90 minutes, but in the end lasted 453 hours. Over 50,000 people appeared on television and more than 10,000 families were reunited. The unexpected impact of the broadcast created new hope for reuniting families separated by the DMZ, and although the North Korean reception was initially unenthusiastic, in 1985, following Red Cross talks at the DMZ, fifty people from each side were allowed to cross the border to hold family reunions. This practice has continued sporadically, except when political tensions between the two Koreas are high.

In recent years, however, increasing numbers of Koreans, especially in the South, have begun to lose interest in the idea of reunification and even to oppose it. This is best characterized in *Meeting with My Brother*, a 1994 novella by Yi Mun-yol published in English translation in 2019. The poignant story, a veiled memoir, is about a South Korean professor who arranges to meet his half-brother, a North Korean, in China. The professor had longed, for many years, to meet his father, who had abandoned his family and defected to the North at the beginning of the Korean War. But after many failed arrangements, his father had died, and he was left to meet with his half-brother, the eldest son in their father's second family. In the course of the novella, several characters serve as conduits for the spectrum of attitudes regarding reunification, which Yi examines as a complex, protracted and possibly disastrous event for both Koreas. On the one hand, reunification could create unmanageable economic liability for the South. On the other hand, the capitalist exploitation of the underdeveloped North could result in a plundering of natural resources, land grabs and the exploitation of cheap labour. Even the many cultural and linguistic differences, exacerbated by more than half a century of division, would be likely to create major social problems in the reunified Korea.

A unified Korean peninsula could also potentially destabilize relationships between the global superpowers. What if a unified democratic Korea, with political pressure from factions maintaining the current interests of the North, were to shift its allegiance from the United States to China, creating a major blow to US security in the Pacific Rim? Such questions have significantly cooled the dream of reunification, particularly for the younger generations that have no direct memory of the horrors of the Korean War and are preoccupied with the pressing problems of the new era: climate change, the declining birth rate, the potential economic threat of AI and the escalating threat of nuclear war. Reunification may remain a dream, but it is not the hopeful dream of the older generations. Perhaps it will become a new guiding myth for the Korean people.

Timeline

Ancient Korea: Gojoseon *c.* 2333 BCE–108 BCE

Gojoseon (고조선 / 古朝鮮, ancient Joseon) was the first kingdom of the Korean peninsula. Its beginnings and the probable extent of its borders are known only through legends, but its existence is corroborated by Chinese histories. In 108 BCE, Emperor Wu of the Chinese Han dynasty conquered Gojoseon and divided it into four commanderies (a way to split up territories into prefectures and put them under Chinese administration).

The Three Kingdoms *c.* 1st century BCE–7th century CE

After the Korean kingdom of Goguryeo (고구려 / 高句麗, 'High and Beautiful') overtook the four Chinese commanderies, the Three Kingdoms period began. In this era, the Korean peninsula was divided into three main kingdoms: Goguryeo, Baekje (백제 / 百濟, 'Hundred Countries') and Silla (신라 / 新羅, literally 'New Gathering', which likely refers to a confederation). Together they controlled not only the peninsula, but also roughly half of what is Manchuria today.

Unified (Great) Silla 7th–10th centuries

The kingdom of Silla unified the Korean peninsula under the Great Silla dynasty. This was a 'golden age' of art and culture. Buddhism flourished in the country, leading to the construction of numerous temples.

Goryeo 918–1392

The Goryeo dynasty succeeded the Unified Silla.

1231–1259:   Mongol invasions of Korea.

1270–1350s: Korean is under the rule of the Mongol Yuan dynasty. This period came to an end as the Yuan dynasty crumbled and the Korean Goryeo dynasty pushed Yuan garrisons out of the peninsula.

1392: The Goryeo dynasty is replaced by the Joseon dynasty after a successful rebellion led by General Yi Seong-gye, who becomes King Taejo, founder of the Korean Yi dynasty, now known as Joseon.

Joseon 1392–1910

The Joseon dynasty rules Korea for over five centuries.

1443: Invention of the Korean script, *hangul*, under King Sejong the Great.

1592–1598: Japanese invasions of Korea (Imjin War).

1627–1637: Manchu invasions of Joseon lead to the decline of the dynasty.

Late 19th century: Western influence and modernization efforts.

Late 19th century: Korea becomes the target of imperial ambitions by Japan, China and Russia.

1910: Korea is annexed by Japan, marking the beginning of the Japanese colonial era.

Post-Second World War and Division into North and South

1945: Korea is liberated from Japanese rule at the end of the Second World War. This period is known as Post-Liberation.

1945–1948: The Korean Peninsula is divided along the 38th parallel into two occupation zones by the United States and the Soviet Union.

1948: The Republic of Korea (South Korea) is established in the US zone, while the Democratic People's Republic of Korea (North Korea) is established in the Soviet zone.

1950–1953: The Korean War breaks out, devastating the entire peninsula. It ends in a ceasefire with the continued division of North and South Korea along the 38th parallel.

Cold War and Modern Era

Both North and South Korea experience rapid economic development and modernization. Between the end of the Korean War in 1953 and the beginning of South Korea's rapid industrialization in the 1970s, North Korea had a higher standard of living for the average person.

1979:   The assassination of President Park Chung-hee and the beginning of the tumultuous decade that would eventually end military dictatorship in South Korea.

1980:   The Gwangju Uprising and the massacre of civilian protesters by the South Korean military under the rule of Chun Doo-hwan marks a turning point in South Koreans' attitude towards the United States, which until that time was almost universally positive.

1988:   After much anticipation and preparation, South Korea hosts the Summer Olympics, marking a turning point in Korea's global presence.

1991:   Both Koreas join the United Nations.

1994:   The death of Kim Il-sung, who posthumously becomes 'Eternal President' of North Korea.

1994–1998:   The 'Arduous March', a period of major economic crisis in North Korea following the collapse of the Soviet Union. Millions starve to death because of famine and drought.

2000:   President Kim Dae-jung wins the Nobel Peace Prize.

2006–present: Ongoing tensions between North and South Korea, including nuclear developments in North Korea.

2017:   The 11th president of South Korea, Park Geun-hye, daughter of Park Chung-hee, is impeached, convicted on charges of corruption, and sentenced to twenty-five years in prison. She is pardoned in 2021 by President Moon Jae-in.

BIBLIOGRAPHY

Armstrong, B.J. 'The United States and Korea: Rediscovering Artifacts of the Naval Past', *War on the Rocks*, 17 January 2018.

Adams, Tim. 'K-Everything: The rise and rise of Korean Culture', *The Guardian*, 4 September 2020.

Bandi (translated by Heinz Insu Fenkl). *The Red Years: Forbidden Poems from Inside North Korea*. London: Zed Books, 2019.

Berg, Sebastian. *Korean Mythology: Folklore and Legends from the Korean Peninsula*. Creek Ridge Publishing, 2022.

Brother Anthony of Taizé (ed.). *Eerie Tales from Old Korea*. Seoul: Seoul Selection, 2013.

Cain, Geoffrey. 'Soap Opera Diplomacy: North Koreans Crave Banned Videos', *Time*, 29 October 2009.

Cawley, Kevin N. (edited by Edward N. Zalta). 'Korean Confucianism', *The Stanford Encyclopedia of Philosophy*, Winter 2021.

Cha, Victor. *The Impossible State: North Korea, Past and Future*. New York: HarperCollins, 2012.

Chae Kyeong-weon (script) & Bae In-Yeong (art) (translated by Bella Dalton-Fenkl). 'The Sea Girl & the Prince', *Words Without Borders*, 2016.

Cho Hak-rae (script) & Pak Chang-yun (art) (translated by Heinz Insu Fenkl). 'How Kim Seon-dal Sold the Water of the Daedong River', *Asia Literary Review*, vol. 23, Spring 2012.

Cho Hak-rae (script) & Ri Chŏl-gun (art) (translated by Heinz Insu Fenkl and Geesu Lee). 'Blizzard in the Jungle', *Words Without Borders*, 2009.

Cho Pyong-won (translated by Heinz Insu Fenkl). 'Great General Mighty Wing (excerpt)', *AZALEA: Journal of Korean Literature & Culture*, vol. 2, Fall 2008.

Choi, In-hak. *A Type Index of Korean Folktales*. Seoul: Myong Ji University Publishing, 1978.

Choi Won-oh.『창세신화 나타난 신화적 사유의 재현과 변주 - 창세, 홍수, 문화의 신화적연관성을 통해』*Reproduction and Variation of Mythical Thinking in the Creation Myth: Through the Mythical Connection of Creation, Flood, and Culture*. Korean Language Education Association, vol. 111, 2003.

Chung Myung-sub et. al. (eds). *Encyclopedia of Korean Folk Literature. Encyclopedia of Korean Folklore and Traditional Culture Vol. III*. Seoul: National Folk Museum of Korea, 2014.

Deuchler, Martina. *The Confucian Transformation of Korea: A Study of Society and Ideology*. Cambridge and London: Harvard University Press, 1992.

Fenkl, Heinz Insu. 'The Blindman's Daughter: Shimch'ong and Other Virtuous Women', *Realms of Fantasy*, February 1999.

——. 'Dangerous Women: Fox Demons to Lilith', *Realms of Fantasy*, April 1999.

——. *Korean Folktales*. Poughkeepsie, NY: Bo-Leaf Books, 2010.

——. 'Tyll Eulenspiegel & Kim Sondal', *Realms of Fantasy*, Summer 2007.

——. 'Reflections on Shamanism and Synthesis', in *New Spiritual Homes: Religion and Asian Americans*, edited by David K. Yoo. University of Hawaii Press, 1999.

——. 'Virtuous Bees: The Culture of North Korean Comics', *Korean Quarterly*, Winter 2010.

Grayson, James Huntley. *Myths and Legends from Korea: An Annotated Compendium of Ancient and Modern Materials*. London and New York: Routledge, 2001.

Griffis, William Elliot. *Korean Fairy Tales.* New York: Thomas Y. Crowell Company, 1922.

Ha Tae Hung. *Folk Tales of Old Korea.* Korean Cultural Series, vol. VI. Seoul: Yonsei University Press, 1958.

Hallyu: From K-Pop to K-Culture.『한류 K-Pop에서 K-Culture로』. Seoul: The Ministry of Culture, Sport, and Tourism and the Korean Culture and Information Service, 2012.

Heo Jeong-sik.『한국의 창조신화 연구, 창세가와 천지왕본풀이를 중심으로』 'A Study of Korea's Creation Myths, Focusing on Genesis and Kings of Heaven and Earth', Woosuk University master's thesis, 1997.

Hong, Euny. *The Birth of Korean Cool: How One Nation is Conquering the World Through Pop Culture.* New York: Picador, 2014.

Hong, Man-jong (translated by Dal-Yong Kim). *Miracles in Korea.* American University Studies Series VII, Theology and Religion, vol. 306. Peter Lang, 2011.

Hyun Yongjun.『제주도무속자료사전』 *Jeju Island Shamanism Data Dictionary.* Shingu Munhwasa, 1980.

Ilyon (edited and translated by Ha Tae-Hung). *Samguk Yusa: Legends & History of the Three Kingdoms of Ancient Korea.* Seoul: Yonsei University Press, 2006.

Im Bang & Yi Ryuk (translated by James S. Gale). *Korean Folk Tales: Imps, Ghosts, and Fairies.* Tokyo: Charles E. Tuttle Co., 1962.

International Cultural Foundation. *Korean Folk Tales.* Korean Culture Series 7. Seoul: Si-sa-yong-o-sa Publishers, Inc., 1982.

Kendall, Laurel. *Shamans, Nostalgias, and the IMF: South Korean Popular Religion in Motion.* Honolulu: University of Hawai'i Press, 2009.

——. *Shamans, Housewives, and Other Restless Spirits: Women in Korean Ritual Life.* Honolulu: University of Hawai'i Press, 1987.

Kim, Anselm K. (ed.). *Korean Religions in Relation: Buddhism, Confucianism, Christianity.* Albany, NY: State University of New York Press, 2016.

Kim Heon-sun.『한국과 유구의 창세신화 비교 연구 - 미륵과 석가의 대결 신화소를 중심으로』 *Comparative Study of Korea and Yugu's Creation Myths: Focusing on the Myth of the Confrontation between Maitreya and Buddha.* Korean Classical Society, 2002.

Kim, Joshua. 'What superstitions and urban myths exist in North Korea?', *Ask a North Korean, NK News,* 4 July 2022.

Kim Man-jung (translation and introduction by Heinz Insu Fenkl). *The Nine Cloud Dream.* Penguin Classics, 2019.

Kim So-un (translated by Higashi Setsu). *The Story Bag: A Collection of Korean Folktales.* Tokyo: Charles E. Tuttle Co., 1955.

Kim Yŏng-sam (script), Ha Chŏng-a (art) (translated by Heinz Insu Fenkl). 'The Crystal Key', *Korean Quarterly,* 2006–2008.

Kim Young-il.『한국무속과 신화의 연구』 *Research on Korean Shamanism and Mythology.* Sejong Publishing House, 2005.

Kim Youngmin & Michael J. Pettid (eds). *Women and Confucianism in Chosŏn Korea: New Perspectives.* Albany, NY: State University of New York Press, 2011.

Koehler, Robert. *Religion in Korea: Harmony and Coexistence.* Korea Essentials 10. Seoul: Seoul Selection, 2010.

Koh Byung-joon. 'N. Korea's myth-making approach shows signs of change under young leader: experts', *Yonhap New Agency, All News,* 11 March 2019.

Lee, Jean H. 'Parsing the propaganda: What to make of Kim Jong Un on a white horse', *The Wilson Center Asia Dispatches,* 29 October 2019.

Lee Jiyoung.『한국의 신화 이야기』 *The Story of Korean Myths.* Sagunja, 2003.

ーー.『창세시조신화의 전승변이에 관한 연구』 *On Transition and Variation of the Myth of the Founder of the Creation.* Research on Korean Language and Literature, Gwanak Language and Literature Research, 1993.

Lee Kyungduk.『창세기와 천지왕본풀이』 *Genesis and the Origin of the King of Heaven and Earth.* 21st Century Books, 2013.

Lee, Peter H. (ed.) (compiled by Seo Daeseok). *Myths of Korea.* Korean Studies Series 4. Seoul: Jimoondang, 2000.

ーー. (ed.) (compiled by Seo Daeseok). *Oral Literature of Korea.* Korean Studies Series 31. Seoul: Jimoondang, 2005.

Lim Seok-jae.『관북지방무가(추가)』 *Gwanbuk Local Shaman Song* (Addendum). Cultural Heritage Administration, 1966.

Martin, Bradley K. *Under the Loving Care of the Fatherly Leader: North Korea and the Kim Dynasty.* Thomas Dunne Books, 2004.

Martin, David L., Commander USN & Nastri, Anthony D., Major USMC. 'The Foot of a Duck', *Proceedings*, vol. 103/4/890, April 1977. *US Naval Institute.*

Mason, David A. *David A. Mason's Sanshin Website.* 2023.

McNeill, David. 'How myths and lies created a nation in thrall to its leader', *The Independent*, 20 December 2011.

Min, Anselm K. (ed.). *Korean Religions in Relation: Buddhism, Confucianism, Christianity.* Albany, NY: SUNY Press, 2016.

Mok Yong Jae & Eugene Whong (translated by Leejin Jun). 'North Korean Founder Kim Il Sung Did Not Have the Ability to Teleport, State Media Admits', *Radio Free Asia*, 22 May 2020.

Musan Cho Oh-hyun (translated by Heinz Insu Fenkl, illustrated by Bella Dalton-Fenkl). 'The Otter and the Hunter', *SIJO: an international journal of poetry and song*, Fall 2019.

Musan Cho Oh-hyun (translated by Heinz Insu Fenkl). *Tales from the Temple.* New Paltz, NY: Codhill Press, 2019.

Ŏm Chŏng-hui (script), Ko Im-hong (art) (translated by Heinz Insu Fenkl and Jungbin Yoon). 'The Secret of Frequency A', *Words Without Borders*, 2011.

Onishi Norimitsu. 'What's Korean for "Real Man"? Ask a Japanese Woman', *The New York Times*, 12 December 2004.

Park, Jongsung. 'Song of the Creation of the Universe', *Encyclopedia of Korean Folk Culture*. National Folk Museum of Korea, 2019.

Park Yong-gun (ed.). *Traditional Tales of Old Korea* (5 vols). Seoul: Hanguk Munhwa Publishing Co., 1975.

Pihl, Marshall R. *The Korean Singer of Tales.* Boston: Harvard University Press, 1994.

Riordan, James. *Korean Folk-tales.* Oxford Myths & Legends Series. New York: Oxford University Press, 1994.

Russell, Mark. *Pop Goes Korea.* Berkeley: Stone Bridge Press, 2009.

Ryang, Sonia. *Reading North Korea: An Ethnological Inquiry.* Harvard East Asian Monographs 341. Cambridge, MA: Harvard University Press, 2012.

Seo Dae-seok.『한국 신화의 연구』 *Research on Korean Mythology.* Jimoondang, 2001.

Yi Mun-yol (translated by Heinz Insu Fenkl and Yoosup Chang). *Meeting with My Brother.* New York: Columbia University Press, 2017.

Zong, In-sob. *Folk Tales from Korea.* London: Routledge & Kegan Paul, 1952.

ACKNOWLEDGMENTS

My deepest gratitude to the many people who helped me learn the Korean that allowed me to write this book: Claire Jungran Kang, whose Korean class I attended at Vassar; and my tutors and friends, Sulgi Koo, Jungbin Yoon, Eunkyo Cho, Lily Kim, Geesu Lee, Scarlet Choi and David Lee. I would like to thank the staff of Vassar College's Frances Lehman Loeb Art Center, including Margaret Vetare, Elizabeth Nogrady, Patricia Phagan, Mary-Kay Lombino and Francine Brown, for the years I spent with the opportunities to learn, up-close, about art throughout the ages, and to educate others about it. I would also like to thank the Art History professors whose guidance prepared me for the research required in writing this book – Brian Lukacher, Susan Donahue Kuretsky – and Jin Xu, who generously shared objects from his Asian art collection for me and my fellow students to study. Special thanks also to Professors Ron Patkus, Marc Epstein, Peter Antelyes, Michael Joyce, Farida Tcherkassova and David Means. I am, as always, grateful to my partner, Lukas Roselle, who has supported me for years and acted as my first reader and cheerleader throughout this process!

BELLA MYŎNG-WŎL DALTON-FENKL

There are many people to thank: Walter Fairservis, who introduced me to the formal study of folk tales; Frederick Carriere, for his generous support and the gift of many volumes of obscure Korean folklore; Peter H. Lee, for recommending me as the translator of *The Nine Cloud Dream*, and for the opportunity to contribute to the *Oral Literature of Korea* volume; Musan Cho Oh-hyun, for illuminating the convergence of languages in his poetry; Kwon Youngmin, for his continued support and encouragement with the study of Buddhist literature; Lee Young-Jun, for inviting me to guest edit the North Korea issue of *AZALEA*; Stephen Wunrow and Martha Vickery at the *Korean Quarterly*, for publishing the first major translations of North Korean comics; and the editors at *Words Without Borders*, for featuring excerpts of North Korean graphic novels over the years. Many thanks to Rob McQuilkin, Max Moorhead and Ellie Roppolo at MMQ for their wonderful support. And, of course, without Anne to keep the stories and analysis alive and coherent, I do not think I could have done the Story Spirits justice.

HEINZ INSU FENKL

Both of us would like to express our appreciation to Ben Hayes, India Jackson, Jen Moore, Yasmin Garcha and Celia Falconer at Thames & Hudson for giving us the opportunity to work on this project, lending us their expertise, and giving us the freedom to earnestly express our thoughts.

SOURCES OF ILLUSTRATIONS

l = left; **r** = right

Roland and Sabrina Michaud/akg-images **206**; The Protected Art Archive/Alamy Stock Photo **11**; CPA Media Pte Ltd/Alamy Stock Photo **25l**; Christian Kober 1/Alamy Stock Photo **39**; Album/Alamy Stock Photo **46**; The History Collection/Alamy Stock Photo **60**; Godong/Alamy Stock Photo **81**; Hakbong Kwon/Alamy Stock Photo **93**; JIPEN/Alamy Stock Photo **116**; David Parker/Alamy Stock Photo **167**; Collection Christophel © Myung film/Alamy Stock Photo **209**; World History Archive/Alamy Stock Photo **214**; Courtesy the authors **64, 88, 168, 184**; © Korean Broadcasting System (KBS); Courtesy the authors **112**; Brooklyn Museum of Art **74**; Ewha Womans University **96**; Anthony Wallace/AFP/Getty Images **172**; Eric Lafforgue/Art In All Of Us/Corbis via Getty Images **159**; Wolfgang Kaehler/LightRocket/ Getty Images **130**; National Diet Library, Japan **137**; Academy of Korean Studies, Jiyoung Kim **107**; Cultural Heritage Administration, Korea **48, 79, 182**; Courtesy Korean Film Archive **164**; Kansong Art Museum, Korea **18**; Digital Image Museum Associates/LACMA/Art Resource NY/Scala, Florence **26**; Mary Evans/Grenville Collins Postcard Collection **133**; National Folk Museum of Korea **30–31, 38, 54, 84, 85, 111, 126, 131, 134, 138, 216**; National Museum of Korea **25r, 34, 57r, 86, 89, 106, 114, 118, 119, 122, 129, 145, 177, 198**; Metropolitan Museum of Art, New York **1, 32, 57l**; Philadelphia Museum of Art **127, 128**; Curioso.Photography/Shutterstock **136**; Jeonghyeon Noh/Shutterstock **50**; magr80/Shutterstock **99**; Tawin Mukdharakosa/Shutterstock **17**; yeouudu/Shutterstock **2**; SuperStock/DeAgostini **212**; Library of Congress, Prints and Photographs Division, Washington, D.C. **58, 63, 100, 117, 152**; 뭘로할까/Wikimedia Commons **92**

INDEX

Page numbers in *italics* refer to illustrations.

Aegukga 222–3
Africa 186–7
Alien Baseball Team 180
Allen, Horace Newton 96
America 183, 191, 192
    films 198, 200
    invasion 100
    naming of 12
    The New Yorker 219
    soldiers 174–6
Amida 84, 85–7, 116
ancestral rituals 92–3, *92, 93*
animism 56–9
April Revolution 191
Arang 143–4, 202
Arduous March 162, 181, 220
'Arirang' 222–4
Aryeong 49–50
aspen *129*, 131
astronomy *30, 31, 50*
Avalokiteshvara 87

Bae Yong-joon 195
baduk 198
Bakgabun 216
Bandi 220–2
Bari, Princess 65–7, 143, 223
Barrett, First Lieutenant Mark 174
Behind Your Touch 205–6
Blackpink 9, 212, 213, 214
Blizzard in the Jungle 186
Bodhidharma 157
bodhisattva 76, 86–7, 144
Bodo League Massacre 190
Bong Joon-ho 196–7, 199
Bonifas, Captain Arthur 174
BTS 9, 213–14
Buddha 29, 78–9, *79*, 80–1, 84, 157
Buddhism 23, 26–7, 28–33, 41, 43–5, 56,
    74, 76–87, *81*, 104, 116, 119, 124
Burning 197

calligraphy 73, 138–9, *138*
Cannes Film Festival 196, 197, 199,
    208, 224
Catholicism 27, 95, 97, 98, 99, 104
centipedes 115
Changsega 28–33
Cheondogyo 23, *99*, 101–4
Cheonjiwang Bonpuri 33–7
Cheomseongdae *50*
Chilseong *74*
chimeras 115–19
Cho Bong-am 191
Cho Pyong-ok 191
Choe Je-u 101
Choe Jun-ho 213
Choi Eun-hee 163–4, 169
Chongmyeong, Lady 35
Christianity 23, 27, 56, 95–9, 101, 155
Chuang Tzu 70
Chumo of Goguryeo 51–3, 118
Chun Doo-hwan 192, 193
Chungnyeol of Goryeo 43
Chunhyang 146–8, 217
civil service exam 89, 91, 135, 148
'The Clever Slave' 134–5
'The Clever Student' 135
Clinton, Bill 171
comic books 45, 178–88
complexion myth 40
Confidential Assignment 208
Confucianism 23, 25–6, 37, 56, 88–95,
    135–6, 144, 146, 189, 217
Confucius 42, 70
cosmetic surgery 215–18
cosmological myths 28, 57
Crash Landing on You 208–10
cultural imperialism 200

Daebyeol 35–6
Daeseji 87
Daesong-dong 176
Dangun Gogi 45
Dangun, King 46–7, *46*, 106, 157
Delisle, Guy 187

Demilitarized Zone (DMZ) 171–8, 224–5
Dharma 80–1, 84
The Disgrace of the Yangban Seongcheon 188
Do Hee-yun 220
dog meat 124
dokkaebi 77, 109, *111*
dolmens 57
donghak ('Eastern Learning') 101
Donghak Peasant Revolt 101–2
Dongmyeong 171
Dragon King 51, 55, 65, 113, 132–5, 140–1, 143
dragons 49, 70, 113–18, *114*, 122
dukka 33, 80

egg ghost 108–9, 217
Eightfold Path 80
Emille Bell 166–7, *167*
'Even Wolves' 123–5
Ewha Womans University 96

fans 69
filial piety 90, 92, 141, 145
Finding Dispersed Families 225
fish 115, 116–17
Five Relationships 90, 93
flag, *Taegeukgi* 24, *25*
foundation myths 40–5, 53–5, 154
Four Noble Truths 32–3, 80
fox figure 94, 109–12, 204–5
French invasion 99–100
frogs 29, 51, 145, *145*
funerary rituals 63, 67, 74
Fuxi 41, 67, 115–16

Gale, James Scarth 98, 105
Ganghwa Island 12, 85, 99–100
'Gangnam Style' 210, 212
gat 205, *206*
gender
  Confucianism 90–1, 93–5
  cosmetic surgery 215–18
  diving women 54–5
  female virtue 139–49
  gumiho 111
  Miss Korea pageant 215–17
  sanshin 107, 108
  Shamanism 61, 62, 65–7

General Sherman 100
Geomun Island 100
Geumwa, King 51
'ghost surgery' 215
ghosts 36, 57, 94, 105–31, 143–4
Gildae, Lady 65
ginseng *131*
girin 118
gisaeng 147–8
'The Goblin's Club' 149–53
Godzilla 163, 168
gogok 57, 58–9, 60
Goguryeo 51–3, 52, 68, 76, 149, 171
Gojoseon 13, 47, 227
Goryeo 14–15, 43, 84, 89, 124, 165, 227–8
Grandma Mago 37, 72
Grandma Seolmundae 37–9
Grandmother Spirit 64
Great General Mighty Wing 181–4, *184*
Great General Spirit 64
Great Silla 26, 227
gukjegyo 8
gumiho 109, 111–12, *112*
gut 61, 62
Gwangju Uprising 192, *193*
Gwanseeum (Gwaneum) *26*, 87
gwishin 107–8
Gyeongdeok, King 166

Habaek 51, 53
Hae Buru, King 51
Hae Mosu 51
Haenyeo 54–5
haetae 89, 117–18, *117*
'Half Moon' 126
Halla, Mount 39, 53
Hallyu 9–10, 194–215, 218–22
han 200–2, 203
Han of the Continent 45
Han Kang 219
Han Sorya 157–8
Hananim 40, 104
Haneullim 104
Hanga 126
Hanguk 14, 201
hangul 15–18, *18*, 98
hanja 15–16, 102, 179
Hibiscus syriacus 129
Hinduism 79–80

Hong Gildong 180
Hong Sang-soo 199
Hsing-chen 82–3
Huibin Jang 94–5
Hwang Dong-hyuk 197
Hwang Hui 135
Hwang Sun-won 123–5
Hwanin 46, 73
Hwanung 46–7
Hyegong, King 166
Hyetong 44
hypergamy 146–8

I Ching 24, 41, 70, 88, 115–16
Im Kwon-taek 199, 224
Imjin War 130, 136–7
Inhyeon, Queen 95
Injong of Goryeo, King 42
instruments, musical 212, 214
Iryeon 41, 43, 45

jade 58, 113
Jade Emperor 72–3
Jang Joon-hwan 202–4
janggu 212, 214
jangseung 58, 59
Japanese 179, 180, 183
    Imjin War 130, 136–7
    rule 18, 24, 97–8, 125, 147, 161, 201,
    224
jayutongil 224–5
Jeju Island 12, 37, 39, 53–4, 56
    Cheonjiwang Bonpuri 33
    diving women 54–5, 54
    Grandma Seolmundae 38–9
    shamans 61, 62
    uprising 190
Jeon Do-yeon 199
Jeon Uchi 73, 75–6
Jesus 78, 98, 102
jige (A-frame) 151, 152, 153
Joint Security Area (JSA) 168, 172,
    174–6
Joseon 13–14, 15, 27, 47, 73, 75–7, 88, 89,
    94–5, 99, 113, 124, 128, 136, 154, 228
JSA: Joint Security Area 207–8, 209
Juche 154, 155, 156, 157–8, 162, 179, 224

K-beauty 215–18
K-drama 195–6, 206

K-pop 210–15
K-Wave *see* Hallyu
kaiju films 163–9
karma 80
Kijong-dong 176–7
Kim Busik 42
Kim Chang-jo 97
Kim Dae-jung 193–4
Kim dynasty 23, 53, 154
Kim Il-sung 13, 102, 155, 156–60, 159,
    161, 169, 170, 171, 174, 181–2, 183,
    186, 194
Kim Jong-il 13, 154, 160–9, 181, 183
Kim Jong-nam 170
Kim Jong-un 13, 154, 156, 160, 169–71,
    181, 207
Kim Ki-duk 199, 208, 224
Kim Man-jung 82
Kim, Patti 211
Kim Seondal 187–8
Kim Sisters 211
Kim Ssangdol 29
Kim Young-sam 193
Kim Yu-mi 215–16
The King of Legend 45
King, Travis 175–6
Ko Un 219
Kongjwi 146, 147
'Koreaboos' 214
Korean People's Army (KPA) 173–5
Korean War 10, 98, 171, 190, 225
Kublai Khan 43

Lao Tzu 69–70
Lee Chang-dong 197, 199, 219
Lee Hyun-se 180
Lee Soo-jung 97
literacy 15–17, 101, 135–6, 179
literature 218–22
longevity symbols 128, 177

MacArthur, Douglas 205–6
magpies 20
magwi/mamul 108
Mahayana Buddhism 29, 76, 77
Maitreya 29
Mandate of Heaven 101
manhwa 180, 181, 182, 184
March 1st Movement 97, 224
martyrs 97–8

mask dance 62–63, *64*
'The Mast of Sand' 135
matriarchy 55
medical tourism 215–16, 217
Meeting with My Brother 225–6
Mireuk 28–33, 84, 85, *86*, 87
Miss Korea pageant 215–17
missionaries 96–9, 101, 105
mogeo 116–17, *116*
moon 29, 35, 36, 49, 73, 102–3, 121, 123,
   126, *127*, 128, 129, 141
   half-moon 126
Moon Byoung-gon 199
moon goddess 126
Moon Jae-in 213
Moon, Sun Myung 102–3
Moonies 102
mountain 9, 11, 16, 29, 32, 37, 38, 46, 47,
   49, 51, 56, 63, 67, 72, 106–7, 108, 120,
   121, 128, 138, 139, 145, 161, 186, 223
muga (shamans' songs) 28–40, 56,
   61–2, 72
Musan Cho Oh-hyun 44

Na Un-gyu 224
Namhae, Crown Prince 50
Neo-Confucianism 88–93, 101, 105,
   149, 153
The New Yorker 219
The Nine Cloud Dream 82, 98
North Korea 10, 12–14, 23, 102, 120,
   154–89, 192, 194, 206–11, 220–6
   comic books 162, 163, 181–7
   famine 160, 162, 182
   Hallyu diplomacy 206–10
   literature 220–2
   reunification 224–6
'The North Wind and the Sun' 194
noses 40

Ogu, King 65, 66–7
Olympic Games 8–9, 120, 124, 179
On the Art of the Cinema 162–3
'Ondal the Fool' 149
onions 130
'Operation Paul Bunyan' 175
origin myths 21, 28–40, 73
otters 44, 178
oxen *81*, 120, 222

Pak Hyeokgeose 47–50
Panmunjom 168, *172*, 173, 174–6
Parasite 196–7, 199
Park Chan-wook 199, 207–8
Park Chung-hee 12, 62, 180, 181, 191, 193
Park Dae-min 188
Park Geun-hye 62
Patjwi 146, 147
peony 31, *32*, *34*
phoenix 118–19, *119*
physiognomy 217
Please Look After Mom 218
Protestantism 27, 97
Pulgasari 163–9
Pure Land Buddhism 77, 85–6, 116
Pyeonggang, Princess 149
Pyongyang: A Journey in North Korea
   187
Pyun Hye-young 219

qi 68–9

rabbits 120, 122, 126–7, *126*, *127*, 129, *134*
'The Rabbit's Judgment' 120, 122
'The Rabbit's Liver' 132–4
'Record of Great Wonders' 43
Red Family 208
red hand 110
red peppers *130*
The Red Years 220
reincarnation 82, 86
reunification 224–6
Ro Tae-woo 192–3
Rodong Sinmun 170

Samguk Sagi 41, 42, 45, 149
Samguk Yusa 41, 43–53, 67
samsara 80
samshin 108
Samshin Halmeoni 108
sanshin 72, 105–6, *106*, *107*, 120
Save the Green Planet! 202–4
Scranton, Mary F. 96
The Secret of Frequency 184–6
Secret Royal Inspector & Joy 205
Secretly Greatly 208
Sejong the Great, King 15–17, *17*, 113
Seo Taiji and Boys 211–12
seohak ('Western Learning') 101

Seok-bong 135, 138–9
Seokga 28–9, 30–3, 79, 84
Seon Buddhism 81–3
Seondal: The Man Who Sells the River
    188
Seowangmo 65
Shamanism 23–4, 28–39, *38*, 55, 56,
    59–67, *60*, 91, 105
Shim Hakkyu 139–43
Shimcheong 139–43, 167, 217
Shin Dong Wu 180
Shin Kyung-sook 218
Shin Sang-ok 163–4, 166–7, 169
shinbyeong ('spirit sickness') 61, 62
Shiri 207, 208
Silla 47–50, *48*, 76, 124, 129
simmani 131
sipu 81
Sobyeol 35–6
Song Kang-ho 199
'Song of the Red People' 221–2
Space Monster Wangmagwi 164, 168
spirits 9, 46, 51, 56, 57, 59–64, 66, 67,
    69, 74, 83, 105–8, 113, 120, 126, *131*, 132,
    141, 144, 146, 150, 173, 205
Squid Game 197
sseseummu 61
stars 13, 19, 29, *31*, 35, 36, *50*, *74*, 119, 124,
    157–8, 161, 169, 171, 206
Steel Rain 208
'The Story Spirits' 132
Sukjong, King 95
Sumyeong Jangja 35–6
sun 13, 24, 29, 35, 36, 49, 51, 73, 102, 121,
    123, 128, 138, 151, 157, 158, 160, 171,
    183, 194
Sunshine Policy 194
syncretism 22, 23, 29, 56, 74, 82, 102,
    198
Syngman Rhee, President 12, 190, 191

taegeuk 24, 25, 58, 71
Taegeukgi 24, 25
talchum ('mask dance') 62–3
The Tale of Chunhyang 146–8
Tales from the Temple 44
Tao Te Ching 68, 69–70
Taoism 23, 24–5, 56, 67–76

Three Kingdoms 41–5, 58, 68, 227
'The Tiger and Persimmon' 121
tigers *20*, 47, 106, 120–3, *122*
trees 32, *38*, 46, 47, 67, 73, 79, 120, 126,
    128, 150, 152, 157, 174–5
'Tree-trimming Incident' 174–5
Tripitaka Koreana 84–5, *84, 85*
turtle ships 136–7, *137*

Uisang 77
Underwood, Horace Grant 96
UNESCO Intangible Cultural Heritage
    55, 223
Ungnyeo 47
Unification Church 102–3
Unified Silla 42, 43, 76, 166
United Nations Command (UNC)
    173–5, 183

The Vegetarian 219

Wei-shu 45
What is Love 195, 196
Winter Sonata 195, 196
wolves 123–5
Wongaksa Pagoda *100*
Wonhyo 77, 109

Yama, King 82
Yang Hyunsuk 212
yangban 91, 95, 188
Yeongjo, King 95
Yeonsangun 17
Yi Mong-ryong 148
Yi Mun-yol 45, 219, 225–6
Yi Sang-sa 144
Yi Seung-hun 95, 97
Yi Su-gwang 95
Yi Sun-sin 136–7, *136*
yin-yang 24, 58, 71, 113, 114, 124
Yongary, Monster from the Deep
    168
Yongbieocheonga 113
Yonsei University 96
Yuhwa 51, 52

Zen 27, 44, 81
Zhu Xi 88, 90, 91